Early Praise for *Distributed Services with Go*

Having built most of the technologies in this book without the benefit of this book, I can wholeheartedly recommend *Distributed Services with Go*. Travis delivers years of practical experience distilled into a clear and concise guide that takes the reader step by step from foundational knowledge to production deployment. This book earns my most hearty endorsement.

➤ **Brian Ketelsen**
Principal Developer Advocate, Microsoft; and Organizer, GopherCon

In this practical, engaging book, Travis Jeffery shines a light on the path to building distributed systems. Read it, learn from it, and get coding!

➤ **Jay Kreps**
CEO, Confluent, Inc., and Co-Creator of Apache Kafka

Travis Jeffery distills the traditionally academic topic of distributed systems down to a series of practical steps to get you up and running. The book focuses on the real-world concepts used every day by practicing software engineers. It's a great read for intermediate developers getting into distributed systems or for senior engineers looking to expand their understanding.

➤ **Ben Johnson**
Author of BoltDB

For any aspiring Gopher, Travis provides a gentle introduction to complex topics in distributed systems and provides a hands-on approach to applying the concepts.

➤ **Armon Dadgar**
HashiCorp Co-Founder

A must-have for Gophers building systems at scale.

➤ **William Rudenmalm**
Lead Developer, CREANDUM

This book is a great resource for Go developers looking to build and maintain distributed systems. It pairs an incremental development process with extensive code examples to teach you how to write your own distributed service, understand how it works under the hood, and how to deploy your service so others may start using it.

➤ **Nishant Roy**
Tech Lead

Distributed Services with Go

Your Guide to Reliable, Scalable, and Maintainable Systems

Travis Jeffery

The Pragmatic Bookshelf

Raleigh, North Carolina

For our complete catalog of hands-on, practical, and Pragmatic content for software developers, please visit *https://pragprog.com*.

The team that produced this book includes:

CEO: Dave Rankin
COO: Janet Furlow
Managing Editor: Tammy Coron
Development Editor: Dawn Schanafelt and Katharine Dvorak
Copy Editor: L. Sakhi MacMillan
Indexing: Potomac Indexing, LLC
Layout: Gilson Graphics
Founders: Andy Hunt and Dave Thomas

For sales, volume licensing, and support, please contact *support@pragprog.com*.

For international rights, please contact *rights@pragprog.com*.

ISBN-13: 978-1-68050-760-7
Book version: P1.0—March 2021

Contents

Part II — Network

Part III — Distribute

Part IV — Deploy

Acknowledgments

I write this, having finished the book, two and a half years after I began. Writing this book was the hardest thing I've done. I've built a few startups and several open source projects—this was much harder. I set out to write a good book people would enjoy and find useful. I'm critical of myself and my work and wouldn't put out anything I didn't deem worthy. It took me a long time to write because I didn't want to compromise. I'm happy with this book and proud of myself.

I thank my editors, Dawn Schanafelt and Katharine Dvorak, for their patience and for helping me to improve my writing and motivating me in hard times.

Thank you to my publisher, The Pragmatic Bookshelf, for the guidance I received in writing my first book and for all of the work out of view.

I thank my book's reviewers and beta readers for giving me their impressions of the book and contributing suggestions and errata to help me improve the book. Thank you to Clinton Begin, Armon Dadgar, Ben Johnson, Brian Ketelsen, Jay Kreps, Nishant Roy, William Rudenmalm, and Tyler Treat.

Thank you to the free and open source software communities for putting out code to study, change, and run. Special thanks to the people at Hashicorp for open-sourcing their Raft and Serf packages I use in this book and their services like Consul, whose source I studied and learned from a lot. Thank you to the Emacs and Linux contributors—the text editor and operating system I wrote this book with. Thank you to the Go team for creating a simple, stable, useful language.

Thank you to my parents, Dave and Tricia Jeffery, for buying my first computer and programming books and encouraging me with a strong work ethic.

Thank you to my high school English teacher, Graziano Galati, for giving me the right reading at the right time in my life.

Thank you to J. R. R. Tolkien for authoring *The Lord of the Rings*. I read it while writing this book, and the rapport with Frodo and Samwise aided me on the journey.

I thank my cat, Callie Jeffery. I adopted her a quarter of the way through writing the book, and her useful contributions to the discussion helped speed up my writing pace.

Thank you to Emily Davidson for her love and support and for fueling me with broccoli soup, ginger kombucha, and matcha tea.

Thank you, dear reader, for independently furthering your skills and knowledge and having the ambition to put your dent in the universe.

—Travis Jeffery

Introduction

Go has become the most popular language for building distributed services, as shown by projects like Docker, Etcd, Vault, CockroachDB, Prometheus, and Kubernetes. Despite the number of prominent projects such as these, however, there's no resource that teaches you why or how you can extend these projects or build your own.

Where do you begin if you want to build a distributed service?

When I began learning how to build distributed services, I found the existing resources to be of two extremes:

- Concrete code—distributed services are large, complex projects, and the prominent ones have had teams working on them for years. The layout of these projects, their technical debt, and their spaghetti code bury the ideas you're interested in, which means you have to dig them out. At best, learning from code is inefficient. Plus there's the risk that you may uncover outdated and irrelevant techniques that you're better off avoiding in your own projects.

- Abstract papers and books—papers and books like *Designing Data-Intensive Applications* by Martin Kleppmann[1] describe how the data structures and algorithms behind distributed services work but cover them as discrete ideas, which means you're left on your own to connect them before you can apply them in a project.

These two extremes leave a chasm for you to cross. I wanted a resource that held my hand and taught me how to build a distributed service—a resource that explained the big ideas behind distributed services and then showed me how to make something of them.

I wrote this book to be that resource. Read this book, and you'll be able to build your own distributed services and contribute to existing ones.

---

1. https://www.oreilly.com/library/view/designing-data-intensive-applications/9781491903063

Who This Book Is For

This book is for intermediate to advanced developers who want to learn how to build distributed services. I've geared the book toward Go programmers, and prior Go experience will help, but you don't have to be an expert. This book shows you how to build distributed services, and the concepts are the same regardless of what language you use. So if you're writing distributed services in Go, you can take full advantage of this book; if not, you can apply the ideas I present here in any language.

This book's code is compatible with Go 1.13+.

What's in This Book

We will design, develop, and deploy a distributed service to explore what Go can do. We'll develop and deploy the service in layers: from the bare essentials of storage handling, to the networking of a client and server, to distributing server instances, deployment, and testing. I divided this book into four parts that parallel those layers. (Don't worry if you aren't familiar with the technologies I mention next—I explain them in the relevant chapters.)

Part I — Get Started

We'll begin with the basic elements: building our project's storage layer and defining its data structures.

In Chapter 1, Let's Go, on page 3, we'll kick off our project by building a simple JSON over HTTP commit log service.

In Chapter 2, Structure Data with Protocol Buffers, on page 13, we'll set up our protobufs, generate our data structures, and set up automation to quickly generate our code as we make changes.

In Chapter 3, Write a Log Package, on page 23, we'll build a commit log library that'll serve as the heart of our service, storing and looking up data.

Part II — Network

This part is where we'll make our service work over a network.

In Chapter 4, Serve Requests with gRPC, on page 55, we'll set up gRPC, define our server and client APIs in protobuf, and build our client and server.

In Chapter 5, Secure Your Services, on page 75, we'll make our connections secure by authenticating our server with SSL/TLS to encrypt data exchanged between client and server and by authenticating requests with access tokens.

In Chapter 6, Observe Your Systems, on page 99, we'll make our service observable by adding logs, metrics, and tracing.

Part III — Distribute

In this part we'll make our service distributed—highly available, resilient, and scalable.

In Chapter 7, Server-to-Server Service Discovery, on page 113, we'll build discovery into our service to make server instances aware of each other.

In Chapter 8, Coordinate Your Services with Consensus, on page 141, we'll add consensus to coordinate the efforts of our servers and turn them into a cluster.

In Chapter 9, Discover Servers and Load Balance from the Client, on page 171, we'll code discovery in our gRPC clients so they discover and connect to the servers with client-side load balancing.

Part IV — Deploy

Here's where we'll deploy our service and make it live.

In Chapter 10, Deploy Applications with Kubernetes Locally, on page 193, we'll set up Kubernetes locally and run a cluster on your local machine. And we'll prepare to deploy to the cloud.

In Chapter 11, Deploy Applications with Kubernetes to the Cloud, on page 219, we'll create a Kubernetes cluster on Google Cloud's Kubernetes Engine and deploy our service to the cloud so that people on the Internet can use it.

If you plan on building the project as you read (which is a great idea), read the parts in order so that your code works. It's also fine to skip around in the book as well; the ideas we'll explore in each chapter have value on their own.

Online Resources

The code we'll develop is available on the Pragmatic Bookshelf website: https://pragprog.com/book/tjgo. You'll also find an errata-submission form there for you to ask questions, report any problems with the text, or make suggestions for future versions of this book.

Let's get *Going*!

Part I

Get Started

CHAPTER 1

Let's Go

Throughout my career I've written programs in C, Ruby, Python, JavaScript, Java, Elixir, Erlang, Bash, and more. Each of these languages had a lot of great things going for it but always at least a few things that bugged me a lot. C didn't have modules, Ruby wasn't fast enough, JavaScript and its type system made you question your sanity, and so on. This meant that each language had a specific use case, like all the different knives a chef uses. For example, a chef uses a cleaver to cut through big bones. Similarly, I'd use Java when writing big, objective-oriented programs and wanted to make a cup of tea between the time I started the program and it was ready to run. A chef uses a paring knife when making small, delicate cuts, and I'd use Bash when writing small, portable scripts. But I always wished I could find a language that was useful in almost all situations and didn't irritate me.

Finally, I came upon Go, a language that can:

- Compile and run your programs faster than an interpreted language like Ruby;
- Write highly concurrent programs;
- Run directly on the underlying hardware; and
- Use modern features like packages (while excluding a lot of features I didn't need, like classes).

Go had more things going for it. So there had to be something that bugged me, right? But no, it was as if the designers of Go had taken all the stuff that bothered me about other languages and stripped them out, leaving the lean, mean programming language that is Go. Go gave me the same feeling that made me first fall in love with programming: that if something was wrong it was my fault, me getting in my way instead of the language burying me under the weight of all its features. If Java is the cleaver and Bash the paring knife, then Go is the katana. Samurai felt that katanas were extensions of themselves, things they could spend a lifetime with while pursuing mastery of their craft. That's the way I feel about Go.

If you were to pick the software field where Go has had the biggest impact, it would have to be distributed systems. The developers of projects like Docker, Kubernetes, Etcd, and Prometheus all decided to use Go for good reason. Google developed Go and its standard library as an answer to software problems at Google: multicore processors, networked systems, massive computation clusters—in other words, distributed systems, and at large scale in terms of lines of code, programmers, and machines. Because you're a Go programmer, you likely use systems like these and want to know how they work, how to debug them, and how to contribute to them, or you want to build similar projects of your own. That's the case for me: the companies I've worked for used Docker and Kubernetes, and I've built my own projects like Jocko, an implementation of Kafka (the distributed commit log) in Go.

So how do you start down the path of knowing how to do all that in Go? Building a distributed service isn't the easiest or smallest project in the world. If you try to build all the pieces at once, all you'll end up with is a big, stinking mess of a code base and a fried brain. You build the project piece by piece. A good place to start is a commit log JSON over HTTP service. Even if you've never written an HTTP server in Go before, I'll teach you how to make an accessible application programming interface (API) that clients can call over the network. You'll learn about commit log APIs and, because we're working on one project throughout this book, you'll be set up to write the code we'll work on in the following chapters.

How JSON over HTTP Services Fits into Distributed Systems

JSON over HTTP APIs are the most common APIs on the web, and for good reason. They're simple to build since most languages have JSON support built in. And they're simple and accessible to use since JSON is human readable and you can call HTTP APIs via the terminal with curl, by visiting the site with your browser, or using any of the plethora of good HTTP clients. If you have an idea for a web service that you want to hack up and have people try as soon as possible, then implementing it with JSON/HTTP is the way to go.

JSON/HTTP isn't limited to small web services. Most tech companies that provide a web service have at least one JSON/HTTP API acting as the public API of their service either for front-end engineers at their company to use or for engineers outside the company to build their own third-party applications on. For their internal web APIs, the company may take advantage of technologies like protobuf for features that JSON/HTTP doesn't provide—like type checking and versioning—but their public one will still be JSON/HTTP for accessibility. This is the same architecture I've used at my current and previous companies. At Segment we had a JSON/HTTP-based architecture that for years handled billions of API calls a month before we changed our internal services to use protobuf/gRPC to improve efficiency. At Basecamp, all services were JSON/HTTP-based and (as far as I know) still are to this day.

JSON/HTTP is a great choice for the APIs of infrastructure projects. Projects like Elasticsearch (a popular open source, distributed search engine) and Etcd (a popular distributed key-value store used by many projects, including Kubernetes) also use JSON/HTTP for their client-facing APIs, while employing their own binary protocols for communication between nodes to improve performance. JSON/HTTP is no toy—you can build all kinds of services with it.

Go has great APIs in its standard library for building HTTP servers and working with JSON, making it perfect for building JSON/HTTP web services. I've worked on JSON/HTTP services written in Ruby, Node.js, Java, Python, and I've found Go to be the most pleasant by far. This is because of the interaction between Go's declarative tags and the great APIs in the JSON encoding package (encoding/json) in the standard library that save you from the fiddling marshaling code you have to write in other languages. So let's dive right in.

Set Up the Project

The first thing we need to do is create a directory for our project's code. Since we're using Go 1.13+, we'll take advantage of modules[1] so you don't have to put your code under your GOPATH. We'll call our project *proglog*, so open your terminal to wherever you like to put your code and run the following commands to set up your module:

```
$ mkdir proglog
$ cd proglog
$ go mod init github.com/travisjeffery/proglog
```

Replace *travisjeffery* with your own GitHub username or with github.com if you use something like Bitbucket, but keep in mind as you're working through this book that the code examples all have github.com/travisjeffery/proglog as the import path, so if you're using your own import path, you must change the code examples to use that import path.

1. https://github.com/golang/go/wiki/Modules

Build a Commit Log Prototype

We'll explore commit logs in depth in Chapter 3, Write a Log Package, on page 23, when we build a persisted commit log library. For now, all you need to know about commit logs is that they're a data structure for an append-only sequence of records, ordered by time, and you can build a simple commit log with a slice.

Create an internal/server directory tree in the root of your project and put the following code under the server directory in a file called log.go:

LetsGo/internal/server/log.go

```
package server

import (
	"fmt"
	"sync"
)

type Log struct {
	mu      sync.Mutex
	records []Record
}

func NewLog() *Log {
	return &Log{}
}

func (c *Log) Append(record Record) (uint64, error) {
	c.mu.Lock()
	defer c.mu.Unlock()
	record.Offset = uint64(len(c.records))
	c.records = append(c.records, record)
	return record.Offset, nil
}

func (c *Log) Read(offset uint64) (Record, error) {
	c.mu.Lock()
	defer c.mu.Unlock()
	if offset >= uint64(len(c.records)) {
		return Record{}, ErrOffsetNotFound
	}
	return c.records[offset], nil
}

type Record struct {
	Value  []byte `json:"value"`
	Offset uint64 `json:"offset"`
}

var ErrOffsetNotFound = fmt.Errorf("offset not found")
```

To append a record to the log, you just append to the slice. Each time we read a record given an index, we use that index to look up the record in the slice. If the offset given by the client doesn't exist, we return an error saying that the offset doesn't exist. All really simple stuff, as it should be since we're using this log as a prototype and want to keep moving.

Ignore Chapter Namespaces in the File Paths

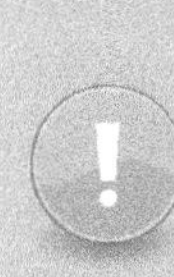

You may have noticed that code snippet's file path said LetsGo/internal/server/log.go instead of internal/server/log.go and that subsequent code snippets have similar per-chapter directory namespaces. These namespaces were needed to structure the code for the book build. When writing your code, pretend that these namespaces don't exist. So for the previous example, the internal directory would go at the root of your project.

Build a JSON over HTTP Server

Now we'll write our JSON/HTTP web server. A Go web server comprises one function—a net/http HandlerFunc(ResponseWriter, *Request)—for each of your API's endpoints. Our API has two endpoints: Produce for writing to the log and Consume for reading from the log. When building a JSON/HTTP Go server, each handler consists of three steps:

1. Unmarshal the request's JSON body into a struct.
2. Run that endpoint's logic with the request to obtain a result.
3. Marshal and write that result to the response.

If your handlers become much more complicated than this, then you should move the code out, move request and response handling into HTTP middleware, and move business logic further down the stack.

Let's start by adding a function for users to create our HTTP server. Inside your server directory, create a file called http.go that contains the following code:

LetsGo/internal/server/http.go

```
package server

import (
	"encoding/json"
	"net/http"

	"github.com/gorilla/mux"
)

func NewHTTPServer(addr string) *http.Server {
	httpsrv := newHTTPServer()
	r := mux.NewRouter()
```

```
        r.HandleFunc("/", httpsrv.handleProduce).Methods("POST")
        r.HandleFunc("/", httpsrv.handleConsume).Methods("GET")
        return &http.Server{
                Addr:    addr,
                Handler: r,
        }
}
```

NewHTTPServer(addr string) takes in an address for the server to run on and returns an *http.Server. We create our server and use the popular gorilla/mux library to write nice, RESTful routes that match incoming requests to their respective handlers. An HTTP POST request to / matches the produce handler and appends the record to the log, and an HTTP GET request to / matches the consume handler and reads the record from the log. We wrap our server with a *net/http.Server so the user just needs to call ListenAndServe() to listen for and handle incoming requests.

Next, we'll define our server and the request and response structs by adding this snippet below NewHTTPServer():

LetsGo/internal/server/http.go

```
type httpServer struct {
        Log *Log
}

func newHTTPServer() *httpServer {
        return &httpServer{
                Log: NewLog(),
        }
}

type ProduceRequest struct {
        Record Record `json:"record"`
}

type ProduceResponse struct {
        Offset uint64 `json:"offset"`
}

type ConsumeRequest struct {
        Offset uint64 `json:"offset"`
}

type ConsumeResponse struct {
        Record Record `json:"record"`
}
```

We now have a server referencing a log for the server to defer to in its handlers. A produce request contains the record that the caller of our API wants appended to the log, and a produce response tells the caller what offset the log stored the records under. A consume request specifies which records the caller of our API wants to read and the consume response to send back those records to the caller. Not bad for just 28 lines of code, huh?

Next, we need to implement the server's handlers. Add the following code below your types from the previous code snippet:

LetsGo/internal/server/http.go

```
func (s *httpServer) handleProduce(w http.ResponseWriter, r *http.Request) {
	var req ProduceRequest
	err := json.NewDecoder(r.Body).Decode(&req)
	if err != nil {
		http.Error(w, err.Error(), http.StatusBadRequest)
		return
	}
	off, err := s.Log.Append(req.Record)
	if err != nil {
		http.Error(w, err.Error(), http.StatusInternalServerError)
		return
	}
	res := ProduceResponse{Offset: off}
	err = json.NewEncoder(w).Encode(res)
	if err != nil {
		http.Error(w, err.Error(), http.StatusInternalServerError)
		return
	}
}
```

The produce handler implements the three steps we discussed before: unmarshaling the request into a struct, using that struct to produce to the log and getting the offset that the log stored the record under, and marshaling and writing the result to the response. Our consume handler looks almost identical. Add the following snippet below your produce handler:

LetsGo/internal/server/http.go

```
func (s *httpServer) handleConsume(w http.ResponseWriter, r *http.Request) {
	var req ConsumeRequest
	err := json.NewDecoder(r.Body).Decode(&req)
	if err != nil {
		http.Error(w, err.Error(), http.StatusBadRequest)
		return
	}
	record, err := s.Log.Read(req.Offset)
	if err == ErrOffsetNotFound {
		http.Error(w, err.Error(), http.StatusNotFound)
		return
	}
	if err != nil {
		http.Error(w, err.Error(), http.StatusInternalServerError)
		return
	}
```

```
	res := ConsumeResponse{Record: record}
	err = json.NewEncoder(w).Encode(res)
	if err != nil {
		http.Error(w, err.Error(), http.StatusInternalServerError)
		return
	}
}
```

The consume handler is like the produce handler but calls Read(offset uint64) to get the record stored in the log. This handler contains more error checking so we can provide an accurate status code to the client if the server can't handle the request, like if the client requested a record that doesn't exist.

That's all the code needed for our server. Now let's write some code to turn your server library into a program we can execute.

Run Your Server

The last code you need to write is a main package with a main() function to start your server. In the root directory of your project, create a cmd/server directory tree, and in the server directory create a file named main.go with this code:

LetsGo/cmd/server/main.go

```
package main

import (
	"log"

	"github.com/travisjeffery/proglog/internal/server"
)

func main() {
	srv := server.NewHTTPServer(":8080")
	log.Fatal(srv.ListenAndServe())
}
```

Our main() function just needs to create and start the server, passing in the address to listen on (localhost:8080) and telling the server to listen for and handle requests by calling ListenAndServe(). Wrapping our server with the *net/http.Server in NewHTTPServer() saved us from writing a bunch of code here—and anywhere else we'd create an HTTP server.

It's time to test our slick new service.

Test Your API

You now have a functioning JSON/HTTP commit log service you can run and test by hitting the endpoints with curl. Run the following snippet to start the server:

```
$ go run main.go
```

Open another tab in your terminal and run the following commands to add some records to your log:

```
$ curl -X POST localhost:8080 -d \
    '{"record": {"value": "TGV0J3MgR28gIzEK"}}'
$ curl -X POST localhost:8080 -d \
    '{"record": {"value": "TGV0J3MgR28gIzIK"}}'
$ curl -X POST localhost:8080 -d \
    '{"record": {"value": "TGV0J3MgR28gIzMK"}}'
```

Go's encoding/json package encodes []byte as a base64-encoding string. The record's value is a []byte, so that's why our requests have the base64 encoded forms of Let's Go #1–3. You can read the records back by running the following commands and verifying that you get the associated records back from the server:

```
$ curl -X GET localhost:8080 -d '{"offset": 0}'
$ curl -X GET localhost:8080 -d '{"offset": 1}'
$ curl -X GET localhost:8080 -d '{"offset": 2}'
```

Congratulations—you have built a simple JSON/HTTP service and confirmed it works!

What You Learned

In this chapter, we built a simple JSON/HTTP commit log service that accepts and responds with JSON and stores the records in those requests to an in-memory log. Next, we'll use protocol buffers to manage our API types, generate custom code, and prepare to write a service with gRPC—an open source, high-performance remote procedure call framework that's great for building distributed services.

CHAPTER 2

Structure Data with Protocol Buffers

When building distributed services, you're communicating between the services over a network. To send data (such as your structs) over a network, you need to encode the data in a format to transmit, and lots of programmers choose JSON. When you're building public APIs or you're creating a project where you don't control the clients, JSON makes sense because it's accessible—both for humans to read and computers to parse. But when you're building private APIs or building projects where you *do* control the clients, you can make use of a mechanism for structuring and transmitting data that—compared to JSON—makes you more productive and helps you create services that are faster, have more features, and have fewer bugs.

So what is this mechanism? Protocol buffers (also known as *protobuf*), which is Google's language and platform-neutral extensible mechanism for structuring and serializing data. The advantages of using protobuf are that it:

- Guarantees type-safety;
- Prevents schema-violations;
- Enables fast serialization; and
- Offers backward compatibility.

Protobuf lets you define how you want your data structured, compile your protobuf into code in potentially many languages, and then read and write your structured data to and from different data streams. Protocol buffers are good for communicating between two systems (such as microservices), which is why Google used protobuf when building gRPC to develop a high-performance remote procedure call (RPC) framework.

If you haven't worked with protobuf before, you may have some of the same concerns I had—that protobuf seems like a lot of extra work. I promise you that, after working with it in this chapter and the rest of the book, you'll see that it's really not so bad. It offers many advantages over JSON, and it'll end up saving you a lot of work.

Here's a quick example that shows what protocol buffers look like and how they work. Imagine you work at Twitter and one of the object types you work with are Tweets. Tweets, at the very least, comprise the author's message. If you defined this in protobuf, it would look like this:

StructureDataWithProtobuf/example.proto

```
syntax = "proto3";

package twitter;

message Tweet {
  string message = 1;
}
```

You'd then compile this protobuf into code in the language of your choice. For example, the protobuf compiler would take this protobuf and generate the following Go code:

StructureDataWithProtobuf/example.pb.go

```
// Code generated by protoc-gen-go. DO NOT EDIT.
// source: example.proto

package twitter

type Tweet struct {
        Message string `protobuf:"bytes,1,opt,name=message,proto3"
json:"message,omitempty"`
        // Note: Protobuf generates internal fields and methods
        // I haven't included for brevity.
}
```

But why not just write that Go code yourself? Why use protobuf instead? I'm glad you asked.

Why Use Protocol Buffers?

Protobuf offers all kinds of useful features:

Consistent schemas
: With protobuf, you encode your semantics once and use them across your services to ensure a consistent data model throughout your whole system. My colleagues and I built the infrastructures at my last two companies on microservices, and we had a repo called "structs" that housed our protobuf and their compiled code, which all our services depended on. By doing this, we ensured that we didn't send multiple, inconsistent schemas to prod. Thanks to Go's type checking, we could update our structs dependency, run the tests that touched our data models, and the

compiler and tests would tell us whether our code was consistent with our schema.

Versioning for free

One of Google's motivations for creating protobuf was to eliminate the need for version checks and prevent ugly code like this:

StructureDataWithProtobuf/example.go

```
if (version == 3) {
...
} else if (version > 4) {
    if (version == 5) {
        ...
    }
    ...
}
```

Think of a protobuf message like a Go struct because when you compile a message it turns into a struct. With protobuf, you number your fields on your messages to ensure you maintain backward compatibility as you roll out new features and changes to your protobuf. So it's easy to add new fields, and intermediate servers that need not use the data can simply parse it and pass through it without needing to know about all the fields. Likewise with removing fields: you can ensure that deprecated fields are no longer used by marking them as reserved; the compiler will then complain if anyone tries to use to the deprecated fields.

Less boilerplate

The protobuf libraries handle encoding and decoding for you, which means you don't have to handwrite that code yourself.

Extensibility

The protobuf compiler supports extensions that can compile your protobuf into code using your own compilation logic. For example, you might want several structs to have a common method. With protobuf, you can write a plugin to generate that method automatically.

Language agnosticism

Protobuf is implemented in many languages: since Protobuf version 3.0, there's support for Go, C++, Java, JavaScript, Python, Ruby, C#, Objective C, and PHP, and third-party support for other languages. And you don't have to do any extra work to communicate between services written in different languages. This is great for companies with various teams that want to use different languages, or when your team wants to migrate to another language.

Performance
: Protobuf is highly performant, and has smaller payloads and serializes up to six times faster than JSON.[1]

gRPC uses protocol buffers to define APIs and serialize messages; we'll use gRPC to build our client and server.

Hopefully I've done a decent job of convincing you that protobuf is cool. But the theory alone is boring! Let's get you set up to create your own protobuf and use it to build stuff.

Install the Protocol Buffer Compiler

The first thing we need to do to get you compiling protobuf is—you guessed it—install the compiler. Go to the Protobuf release page on GitHub[2] and download the relevant release for your computer. If you're on a Mac, for instance, you'd download protoc-3.9.0-osx-x86_64.zip. You can download and install in your terminal like so:

```
$ wget https://github.com/protocolbuffers/protobuf/\
releases/download/v3.9.0/protoc-3.9.0-osx-x86_64.zip
$ unzip protoc-3.9.0-osx-x86_64.zip -d /usr/local/protobuf
```

Here's what the layout and files in the extracted protobuf directory look like:

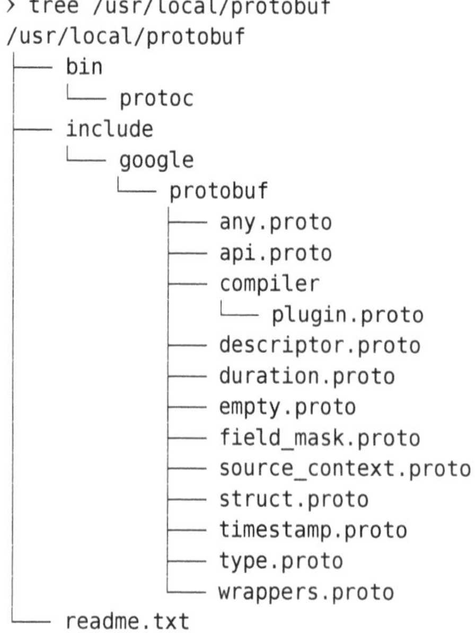

```
> tree /usr/local/protobuf
/usr/local/protobuf
├── bin
│   └── protoc
├── include
│   └── google
│       └── protobuf
│           ├── any.proto
│           ├── api.proto
│           ├── compiler
│           │   └── plugin.proto
│           ├── descriptor.proto
│           ├── duration.proto
│           ├── empty.proto
│           ├── field_mask.proto
│           ├── source_context.proto
│           ├── struct.proto
│           ├── timestamp.proto
│           ├── type.proto
│           └── wrappers.proto
└── readme.txt
```

1. https://auth0.com/blog/beating-json-performance-with-protobuf
2. https://github.com/protocolbuffers/protobuf/releases

As you can see, a protobuf installation consists of two directories. The bin directory contains the compiler binary named protoc, and the include directories contains a bunch of protobuf files that are like protobuf's standard library. A mistake I've seen many people make when setting up their systems to work with protobuf is that they install the compiler binary without the include protobuf files. But without those files you can't compile successfully, so just extract the whole release using the commands I just showed you and you'll be just dandy.

Now that you've got the compiler binary installed, make sure your shell can find and run it. Add the binary to your PATH env var using your shell's configuration file. If you're using ZSH for instance, run something like the following to update your configuration:

```
$ echo 'export PATH="$PATH:/usr/local/protobuf/bin"' >> ~/.zshenv
```

At this point the protobuf compiler is installed on your machine. To test the installation, run protoc --version. If you don't see any errors, you're ready to handle the rest of this chapter. If you do see errors, don't worry: few installation problems are unique. Google will show you the way.

With the compiler installed, you're ready to write and compile some protobuf. Let's get to it!

Define Your Domain Types as Protocol Buffers

In the previous chapter, we defined our Record type in Go as this struct:

LetsGo/internal/server/log.go

```go
type Record struct {
	Value  []byte `json:"value"`
	Offset uint64 `json:"offset"`
}
```

To turn that into a protobuf message we need to convert the Go code into protobuf syntax.

The convention for Go projects is to put your protobuf in an api directory. So run mkdir -p api/v1 to create your directories, then create a file called log.proto in the v1 directory and put this code in it:

StructureDataWithProtobuf/api/v1/log.proto

```
syntax = "proto3";

package log.v1;

option go_package = "github.com/travisjeffery/api/log_v1";
```

```
message Record {
  bytes value = 1;
  uint64 offset = 2;
}
```

In this protobuf code, we specify that we're using proto3 syntax—the latest version of protobuf syntax. Then we specify a package name for two reasons: because this protobuf package name is used as the package name in the generated Go code and because it prevents name clashes between protocol message types that have the same name.

These protobuf messages are equivalent to the Go structs shown earlier. You'll notice the two syntaxes are very similar: in Go you have struct, and with protobuf you have a message—both with a list of fields. In Go you put the name of the field on the left followed by its type, and with protobuf you put the name of the field on right followed by its name (with an additional field ID).

Following the package declarations in the protobuf code, we define our Record type. Protocol buffer programmers use the repeated keyword to define a slice of some type, so repeated Record records means the records field is a []Record in Go.

I mentioned earlier that one handy feature of protobuf is the ability to version fields. Each field has a type, name, and unique field number. These field numbers identify your fields in the marshaled binary format, and you shouldn't change them once your messages are in use in your projects. Consider fields immutable: you can stop using old fields and add new fields, but you can't modify existing fields. You want to change fields like this when you make small, iterative changes—like when you add or remove features or data from a message.

Besides field versions, you'll also want to group your messages by a major version. The major version gives you control over your protobuf when you overhaul projects to rearchitect your infrastructure or run multiple message versions at the same time for a migration period. Bumping major versions should be a rare occurrence because for most changes, field versioning is sufficient. I've only had to bump the major version of my protobuf twice, and if you look at Google's API definitions[3] protobuf, they've only bumped their major version a couple times. So changing major versions is uncommon, but it's nice to have the ability when you need it.

3. https://github.com/googleapis/googleapis

At the beginning of this section, I had you put the log.proto file into an api/v1 directory. The v1 represents these protobufs' major version. If you were to continue building this project and decided to break API compatibility, you would create a v2 directory to package the new messages together and communicate to your users you've made incompatible API changes.

Now that we've created the protocol buffer messages, let's compile your protobuf into Go code.

Compile Protocol Buffers

To compile protobuf into the code of some programming language, you need the runtime for that language. The compiler itself doesn't know how to compile protobuf into every language—it needs a language-specific runtime to do so.

Go has two runtimes to compile protobuf into Go code. The Go team and the protobuf team at Google developed the original runtime.[4] Then a team of folks who wanted more features forked the original runtime and developed it into gogoprotobuf, with more code-generation features and faster marshaling and unmarshaling. Projects like Etcd, Mesos, Kubernetes, Docker, CockroachDB, and NATS as well as companies like Dropbox and Sendgrid used gogoprotobuf. I used gogoprotobuf for my projects to integrate with Kubernetes' protocol buffers and for gogoprotobuf's features.

In March 2020, the Go team released a major revision of the Go API (APIv2)[5] for protocol buffers with improved performance[6] and a reflection API that enables adding features like those provided by gogoprotobuf. Projects[7] that used gogoprotobuf have begun switching to APIv2[8] because of APIv2's improved performance, its new reflection API, its incompatibility with gogoprotobuf, and the gogoprotobuf project needing new ownership.[9] I recommend using APIv2, too.

To compile our protobuf into Go, we need to install the protobuf runtime by running the following command:

```
$ go get google.golang.org/protobuf/...@v1.25.0
```

4. https://github.com/golang/protobuf
5. https://github.com/alexshtin/proto-bench/blob/master/README.md
6. https://github.com/istio/istio/pull/24956
7. https://github.com/istio/api/pull/1607
8. https://github.com/envoyproxy/go-control-plane/pull/226
9. https://github.com/gogo/protobuf/issues/691

You can now compile your protobuf by running the following command at the root of your project:

```
$ protoc api/v1/*.proto \
        --go_out=. \
        --go_opt=paths=source_relative \
        --proto_path=.
```

Look in the api/v1 directory and you'll see a new file called log.pb.go. Open it up to see the Go code that the compiler generated from your protobuf code. Your protobuf message has been turned into a Go struct, along with some methods on the struct for marshaling to the protobuf binary wire format, and getters for your fields.

Since you'll compile your protobuf every time you change them, it's worth adding a Makefile file with a compile target that you can quickly run again and again. We'll include a test target for testing our code too. So create a Makefile file at the root of your repo with the following code:

StructureDataWithProtobuf/Makefile

```
compile:
	protoc api/v1/*.proto \
		--go_out=. \
		--go_opt=paths=source_relative \
		--proto_path=.

test:
	go test -race ./...
```

That's all there is to compiling your protobuf code into Go code. Now let's talk about how to work with the generated code and extend the compiler to generate your own code.

Work with the Generated Code

Although the generated code in log.pb.go is a lot longer than your handwritten code in log.go (because of the extra code needed to marshal to the protobuf binary wire format), you'll use the code as if you'd handwritten it. For example, you'll create instances using the & operator (or new keyword) and access fields using a dot.

The compiler generates various methods on the struct, but the only methods you'll use directly are the getters. Use the struct's fields when you can, but you'll find the getters useful when you have multiple messages with the same getter(s) and you want to abstract those method(s) into an interface. For example, imagine you're building a retail site like Amazon and have different types of stuff you sell—books, games, and so on—each with a field for the item's price, and you want to find the total of the items in the user's cart. You'd make a Pricer interface and a Total function that takes in a slice of Pricer interfaces and returns their total cost. Here's what the code would look like:

```
type Book struct {
    Price uint64
}

func(b *Book) GetPrice() uint64 { // ... }

type Game struct {
    Price uint64
}

func(b *Game) GetPrice() uint64 { // ... }

type Pricer interface {
    GetPrice() uint64
}

func Total(items []Pricer) uint64 { // ... }
```

Now imagine that you want to write a script to change the price of all your inventory—books, games, and so on. You *could* do this with reflection, but reflection should be your last resort since, as the Go proverb goes, reflection is never clear.[10] If we just had setters, we could use an interface like the following to set the price on the different kinds of items in your inventory:

```
type PriceAdjuster interface {
    SetPrice(price uint64)
}
```

When the compiled code isn't quite what you need, you can extend the compiler's output with plugins. Though we don't need to write a plugin for this project, I've written some plugins that were incredibly useful to the projects I worked on; it's worth learning to write your own so you can recognize when a plugin will save you a ton of manual labor.

What You Learned

In this chapter, we covered the protobuf fundamentals we'll use throughout our project. These concepts will be vital throughout our project, especially as we build our gRPC client and server. Now let's create the next vital piece of our project: a commit log library.

10. https://bit.ly/2HcYojl

CHAPTER 3

Write a Log Package

In this book we're building a distributed service to learn how to create distributed services with Go (shocker). But how does building a log in this chapter help us achieve that goal? I believe the log is the most important tool in your toolkit when building distributed services. Logs—which are sometimes also called *write-ahead logs*, *transaction logs*, or *commit logs*—are at the heart of storage engines, message queues, version control, and replication and consensus algorithms. As you build distributed services, you'll face problems that you can solve with logs. By building a log yourself, you'll learn how to:

- Solve problems using logs and discover how they can make hard problems easier.
- Change existing log-based systems to fit your needs and build your own log-based systems.
- Write and read data efficiently when building storage engines.
- Protect against data loss caused by system failures.
- Encode data to persist it to a disk or to build your own wire protocols and send the data between applications.

And who knows—maybe you'll be the one who builds the next big distributed log service.

The Log Is a Powerful Tool

Folks who develop storage engines of filesystems and databases use logs to improve the data integrity of their systems. The ext filesystems, for example, log changes to a journal instead of directly changing the disk's data file. Once the filesystem has safely written the changes to the journal, it then applies those changes to the data files. Logging to the journal is simple and fast, so there's little chance of losing data. Even if your computer crashed before ext had finished updating the disk files, then on the next boot, the filesystem would process the data in the journal to complete its updates. Database developers, like PostgreSQL, use the same technique to make their systems durable: they record changes to a log, called a write-ahead log (WAL), and later process the WAL to apply the changes to their database's data files.

Database developers use the WAL for replication, too. Instead of writing the logs to a disk, they write the logs over the network to its replicas. The replicas apply the changes to their own data copies, and eventually they all end up at the same state. Raft, a consensus algorithm, uses the same idea to get distributed services to agree on a cluster-wide state. Each node in a Raft cluster runs a state machine with a log as its input. The leader of the Raft cluster appends changes to its followers' logs. Since the state machines use the logs as input and because the logs have the same records in the same order, all the services end up with the same state.

Web front-end developers use logs to help manage state in their applications. In Redux,[1] a popular JavaScript library commonly used with React, you log changes as plain objects and handle those changes with pure functions that apply the updates to your application's state.

All these examples use logs to store, share, and process ordered data. This is really cool because the same tool helps replicate databases, coordinate distributed services, and manage state in front-end applications. You can solve a lot of problems, especially in distributed services, by breaking down the changes in your system until they're single, atomic operations that you can store, share, and process with a log.

Databases often provide a way to restore their state to some time in the past, often referred to as point-in-time recovery. You take a snapshot of your database from the past and then replay the logs from the write-ahead log until it's at the point in time you want. You don't need the snapshot if you have every single log since the beginning to replay, but for databases with long histories and a lot of changes, keeping every log isn't feasible. Redux uses the same idea to undo/redo actions: it logs the application's state after each action and undoing an action just requires Redux to move the state shown in the UI to the previously logged state. Distributed version control systems like Git work similarly; your commit log history is a literal commit log.

---

1. https://redux.js.org

As you can see, a complete log not only holds the latest state, but all states that have existed, which allows you to build some cool features that you'd find complicated to build otherwise. Logs are simple—and that's why they're good.

How Logs Work

A log is an append-only sequence of records. You append records to the end of the log, and you typically read top to bottom, oldest to newest—similar to running `tail -f` on a file. You can log any data. People have historically used the term *logs* to refer to lines of text meant for humans to read, but that's changed as more people use log systems where their "logs" are binary-encoded messages meant for other programs to read. When I talk about logs and records in this book, I'm not talking about any particular type of data. When you append a record to a log, the log assigns the record a unique and sequential offset number that acts like the ID for that record. A log is like a table that always orders the records by time and indexes each record by its offset and time created.

Concrete implementations of logs have to deal with us not having disks with infinite space, which means we can't append to the same file forever. So we split the log into a list of segments. When the log grows too big, we free up disk space by deleting old segments whose data we've already processed or archived. This cleaning up of old segments can run in a background process while our service can still produce to the active (newest) segment and consume from other segments with no, or at least fewer, conflicts where goroutines access the same data.

There's always one special segment among the list of segments, and that's the active segment. We call it the *active* segment because it's the only segment we actively write to. When we've filled the active segment, we create a new segment and make *it* the active segment.

Each segment comprises a store file and an index file. The segment's store file is where we store the record data; we continually append records to this file. The segment's index file is where we index each record in the store file. The index file speeds up reads because it maps record offsets to their position in the store file. Reading a record given its offset is a two-step process: first you get the entry from the index file for the record, which tells you the position of the record in the store file, and then you read the record at that position in the store file. Since the index file requires only two small fields—the offset and stored position of the record—the index file is much smaller than the store file that stores all your record data. Index files are small enough that we can memory-map[2] them and make operations on the file as fast as operating on in-memory data.

Now that you know how logs work, it's time to build our own. Let's get cracking to code it up.

Build a Log

We will build our log from the bottom up, starting with the store and index files, then the segment, and finally the log. That way we can write and run tests as we build each piece. Since the word *log* can refer to at least three different things—a record, the file that stores records, and the abstract data type that ties segments together—to make things less confusing, throughout this chapter, I will consistently use the following terms to mean these things:

- *Record*—the data stored in our log.
- *Store*—the file we store records in.
- *Index*—the file we store index entries in.
- *Segment*—the abstraction that ties a store and an index together.
- *Log*—the abstraction that ties all the segments together.

Code the Store

To get started, create a directory at internal/log for our log package, then create a file called store.go in that directory that contains the following code:

WriteALogPackage/internal/log/store.go

```
package log

import (
	"bufio"
	"encoding/binary"
	"os"
	"sync"
)

var (
	enc = binary.BigEndian
)

const (
	lenWidth = 8
)

type store struct {
	*os.File
```

2. https://en.wikipedia.org/wiki/Memory-mapped_file

```
	mu   sync.Mutex
	buf  *bufio.Writer
	size uint64
}

func newStore(f *os.File) (*store, error) {
	fi, err := os.Stat(f.Name())
	if err != nil {
		return nil, err
	}
	size := uint64(fi.Size())
	return &store{
		File: f,
		size: size,
		buf:  bufio.NewWriter(f),
	}, nil
}
```

The store struct is a simple wrapper around a file with two APIs to append and read bytes to and from the file. The newStore(*os.File) function creates a store for the given file. The function calls os.Stat(name string) to get the file's current size, in case we're re-creating the store from a file that has existing data, which would happen if, for example, our service had restarted.

We refer to the enc variable and lenWidth constant repeatedly in the store, so we place them up top where they're easy to find. enc defines the encoding that we persist record sizes and index entries in and lenWidth defines the number of bytes used to store the record's length.

Next, write the following Append() method below newStore():

WriteALogPackage/internal/log/store.go

```
func (s *store) Append(p []byte) (n uint64, pos uint64, err error) {
	s.mu.Lock()
	defer s.mu.Unlock()
	pos = s.size
	if err := binary.Write(s.buf, enc, uint64(len(p))); err != nil {
		return 0, 0, err
	}
	w, err := s.buf.Write(p)
	if err != nil {
		return 0, 0, err
	}
	w += lenWidth
	s.size += uint64(w)
	return uint64(w), pos, nil
}
```

Append([]byte) persists the given bytes to the store. We write the length of the record so that, when we read the record, we know how many bytes to read.

We write to the buffered writer instead of directly to the file to reduce the number of system calls and improve performance. If a user wrote a lot of small records, this would help a lot. Then we return the number of bytes written, which similar Go APIs conventionally do, and the position where the store holds the record in its file. The segment will use this position when it creates an associated index entry for this record.

Below Append(), add the following Read() method:

WriteALogPackage/internal/log/store.go
```
func (s *store) Read(pos uint64) ([]byte, error) {
	s.mu.Lock()
	defer s.mu.Unlock()
	if err := s.buf.Flush(); err != nil {
		return nil, err
	}
	size := make([]byte, lenWidth)
	if _, err := s.File.ReadAt(size, int64(pos)); err != nil {
		return nil, err
	}
	b := make([]byte, enc.Uint64(size))
	if _, err := s.File.ReadAt(b, int64(pos+lenWidth)); err != nil {
		return nil, err
	}
	return b, nil
}
```

Read(pos uint64) returns the record stored at the given position. First it flushes the writer buffer, in case we're about to try to read a record that the buffer hasn't flushed to disk yet. We find out how many bytes we have to read to get the whole record, and then we fetch and return the record. The compiler allocates byte slices that don't escape the functions they're declared in on the stack. A value escapes when it lives beyond the lifetime of the function call—if you return the value, for example.

Put this ReadAt() method under Read():

WriteALogPackage/internal/log/store.go
```
func (s *store) ReadAt(p []byte, off int64) (int, error) {
	s.mu.Lock()
	defer s.mu.Unlock()
	if err := s.buf.Flush(); err != nil {
		return 0, err
	}
	return s.File.ReadAt(p, off)
}
```

ReadAt(p []byte, off int64) reads len(p) bytes into p beginning at the off offset in the store's file. It implements io.ReaderAt on the store type.

Last, add this Close() method after ReadAt():

WriteALogPackage/internal/log/store.go
```
func (s *store) Close() error {
	s.mu.Lock()
	defer s.mu.Unlock()
	err := s.buf.Flush()
	if err != nil {
		return err
	}
	return s.File.Close()
}
```

Close() persists any buffered data before closing the file.

Let's test that our store works. Create a store_test.go file in the log directory with the following code:

WriteALogPackage/internal/log/store_test.go
```
package log

import (
	"io/ioutil"
	"os"
	"testing"

	"github.com/stretchr/testify/require"
)

var (
	write = []byte("hello world")
	width = uint64(len(write)) + lenWidth
)

func TestStoreAppendRead(t *testing.T) {
	f, err := ioutil.TempFile("", "store_append_read_test")
	require.NoError(t, err)
	defer os.Remove(f.Name())

	s, err := newStore(f)
	require.NoError(t, err)

	testAppend(t, s)
	testRead(t, s)
	testReadAt(t, s)

	s, err = newStore(f)
	require.NoError(t, err)
	testRead(t, s)
}
```

In this test, we create a store with a temporary file and call two test helpers to test appending and reading from the store. Then we create the store again and test reading from it again to verify that our service will recover its state after a restart.

After the TestStoreAppendRead() function, add these test helpers:

WriteALogPackage/internal/log/store_test.go

```
func testAppend(t *testing.T, s *store) {
	t.Helper()
	for i := uint64(1); i < 4; i++ {
		n, pos, err := s.Append(write)
		require.NoError(t, err)
		require.Equal(t, pos+n, width*i)
	}
}

func testRead(t *testing.T, s *store) {
	t.Helper()
	var pos uint64
	for i := uint64(1); i < 4; i++ {
		read, err := s.Read(pos)
		require.NoError(t, err)
		require.Equal(t, write, read)
		pos += width
	}
}

func testReadAt(t *testing.T, s *store) {
	t.Helper()
	for i, off := uint64(1), int64(0); i < 4; i++ {
		b := make([]byte, lenWidth)
		n, err := s.ReadAt(b, off)
		require.NoError(t, err)
		require.Equal(t, lenWidth, n)
		off += int64(n)

		size := enc.Uint64(b)
		b = make([]byte, size)
		n, err = s.ReadAt(b, off)
		require.NoError(t, err)
		require.Equal(t, write, b)
		require.Equal(t, int(size), n)
		off += int64(n)
	}
}
```

Below testReadAt(), add this snippet to test the Close() method:

WriteALogPackage/internal/log/store_test.go

```
func TestStoreClose(t *testing.T) {
	f, err := ioutil.TempFile("", "store_close_test")
	require.NoError(t, err)
	defer os.Remove(f.Name())
	s, err := newStore(f)
```

```
        require.NoError(t, err)
        _, _, err = s.Append(write)
        require.NoError(t, err)

        f, beforeSize, err := openFile(f.Name())
        require.NoError(t, err)

        err = s.Close()
        require.NoError(t, err)

        _, afterSize, err := openFile(f.Name())
        require.NoError(t, err)
        require.True(t, afterSize > beforeSize)
}

func openFile(name string) (file *os.File, size int64, err error) {
        f, err := os.OpenFile(
                name,
                os.O_RDWR|os.O_CREATE|os.O_APPEND,
                0644,
        )
        if err != nil {
                return nil, 0, err
        }
        fi, err := f.Stat()
        if err != nil {
                return nil, 0, err
        }
        return f, fi.Size(), nil
}
```

Assuming these tests pass, you know that your log can append and read persisted records.

Write the Index

Next let's code the index. Create an index.go file inside internal/log that contains the following code:

WriteALogPackage/internal/log/index.go

```
package log

import (
        "io"
        "os"

        "github.com/tysontate/gommap"
)

var (
        offWidth uint64 = 4
        posWidth uint64 = 8
        entWidth        = offWidth + posWidth
)
```

```
type index struct {
	file *os.File
	mmap gommap.MMap
	size uint64
}
```

We use the *Width constants throughout the index, so like with the store's variables and constants, we put the constants at the top of the file to make them easy to find. The *Width constants define the number of bytes that make up each index entry.

Our index entries contain two fields: the record's offset and its position in the store file. We store offsets as uint32s and positions as uint64s, so they take up 4 and 8 bytes of space, respectively. We use the entWidth to jump straight to the position of an entry given its offset since the position in the file is offset * entWidth.

index defines our index file, which comprises a persisted file and a memory-mapped file. The size tells us the size of the index and where to write the next entry appended to the index.

Now add the following newIndex() function below the index:

WriteALogPackage/internal/log/index.go

```
func newIndex(f *os.File, c Config) (*index, error) {
	idx := &index{
		file: f,
	}
	fi, err := os.Stat(f.Name())
	if err != nil {
		return nil, err
	}
	idx.size = uint64(fi.Size())
	if err = os.Truncate(
		f.Name(), int64(c.Segment.MaxIndexBytes),
	); err != nil {
		return nil, err
	}
	if idx.mmap, err = gommap.Map(
		idx.file.Fd(),
		gommap.PROT_READ|gommap.PROT_WRITE,
		gommap.MAP_SHARED,
	); err != nil {
		return nil, err
	}
	return idx, nil
}
```

newIndex(*os.File) creates an index for the given file. We create the index and save the current size of the file so we can track the amount of data in the index file as we add index entries. We grow the file to the max index size before memory-mapping the file and then return the created index to the caller.

Next, add the following Close() method below newIndex():

WriteALogPackage/internal/log/index.go

```
func (i *index) Close() error {
	if err := i.mmap.Sync(gommap.MS_SYNC); err != nil {
		return err
	}
	if err := i.file.Sync(); err != nil {
		return err
	}
	if err := i.file.Truncate(int64(i.size)); err != nil {
		return err
	}
	return i.file.Close()
}
```

Close() makes sure the memory-mapped file has synced its data to the persisted file and that the persisted file has flushed its contents to stable storage. Then it truncates the persisted file to the amount of data that's actually in it and closes the file.

Now that we've seen the code for both opening and closing an index, we can discuss what this growing and truncating the file business is all about.

When we start our service, the service needs to know the offset to set on the next record appended to the log. The service learns the next record's offset by looking at the last entry of the index, a simple process of reading the last 12 bytes of the file. However, we mess up this process when we grow the files so we can memory-map them. (The reason we resize them now is that, once they're memory-mapped, we can't resize them, so it's now or never.) We grow the files by appending empty space at the end of them, so the last entry is no longer at the end of the file—instead, there's some unknown amount of space between this entry and the file's end. This space prevents the service from restarting properly. That's why we shut down the service by truncating the index files to remove the empty space and put the last entry at the end of the file once again. This graceful shutdown returns the service to a state where it can restart properly and efficiently.

Handling Ungraceful Shutdowns

A graceful shutdown occurs when a service finishes its ongoing tasks, performs its processes to ensure there's no data loss, and prepares for a restart. If your service crashes or its hardware fails, you'll experience an ungraceful shutdown. An example of an ungraceful shutdown for the service we're building would be if it lost power before it finished truncating its index files. You handle ungraceful shutdowns by performing a sanity check when your service restarts to find corrupted data. If you have corrupted data, you can rebuild the data or replicate the data from an uncorrupted source. The log we're building doesn't handle ungraceful shutdowns because I wanted to keep the code simple.

And now back to our regularly scheduled programming.

Add the following `Read()` method below `newIndex()`:

WriteALogPackage/internal/log/index.go

```
func (i *index) Read(in int64) (out uint32, pos uint64, err error) {
	if i.size == 0 {
		return 0, 0, io.EOF
	}
	if in == -1 {
		out = uint32((i.size / entWidth) - 1)
	} else {
		out = uint32(in)
	}
	pos = uint64(out) * entWidth
	if i.size < pos+entWidth {
		return 0, 0, io.EOF
	}
	out = enc.Uint32(i.mmap[pos : pos+offWidth])
	pos = enc.Uint64(i.mmap[pos+offWidth : pos+entWidth])
	return out, pos, nil
}
```

`Read(int64)` takes in an offset and returns the associated record's position in the store. The given offset is relative to the segment's base offset; `0` is always the offset of the index's first entry, 1 is the second entry, and so on. We use relative offsets to reduce the size of the indexes by storing offsets as uint32s. If we used absolute offsets, we'd have to store the offsets as uint64s and require four more bytes for each entry. Four bytes doesn't sound like much, until you multiply it by the number of records people often use distributed logs for, which with a company like LinkedIn is *trillions* of records every day. Even relatively small companies can make billions of records per day.

Now add the following Write() method below Read():

WriteALogPackage/internal/log/index.go
```
func (i *index) Write(off uint32, pos uint64) error {
	if uint64(len(i.mmap)) < i.size+entWidth {
		return io.EOF
	}
	enc.PutUint32(i.mmap[i.size:i.size+offWidth], off)
	enc.PutUint64(i.mmap[i.size+offWidth:i.size+entWidth], pos)
	i.size += uint64(entWidth)
	return nil
}
```

Write(off uint32, pos uint32) appends the given offset and position to the index. First, we validate that we have space to write the entry. If there's space, we then encode the offset and position and write them to the memory-mapped file. Then we increment the position where the next write will go.

Add this Name() method to return the index's file path:

WriteALogPackage/internal/log/index.go
```
func (i *index) Name() string {
	return i.file.Name()
}
```

Let's test our index. Create an index_test.go file in internal/log starting with the following code:

WriteALogPackage/internal/log/index_test.go
```
package log

import (
	"io"
	"io/ioutil"
	"os"
	"testing"

	"github.com/stretchr/testify/require"
)

func TestIndex(t *testing.T) {
	f, err := ioutil.TempFile(os.TempDir(), "index_test")
	require.NoError(t, err)
	defer os.Remove(f.Name())

	c := Config{}
	c.Segment.MaxIndexBytes = 1024
	idx, err := newIndex(f, c)
	require.NoError(t, err)
	_, _, err = idx.Read(-1)
	require.Error(t, err)
	require.Equal(t, f.Name(), idx.Name())
```

```
	entries := []struct {
		Off uint32
		Pos uint64
	}{
		{Off: 0, Pos: 0},
		{Off: 1, Pos: 10},
	}
```

This code sets up the test. We create an index file and make it big enough to contain our test entries via the Truncate() call. We have to grow the file before we use it because we memory-map the file to a slice of bytes and if we didn't increase the size of the file before we wrote to it, we'd get an out-of-bounds error.

Finally, add the following code beneath the previous snippet to finish the test:

WriteALogPackage/internal/log/index_test.go

```
	for _, want := range entries {
		err = idx.Write(want.Off, want.Pos)
		require.NoError(t, err)

		_, pos, err := idx.Read(int64(want.Off))
		require.NoError(t, err)
		require.Equal(t, want.Pos, pos)
	}

	// index and scanner should error when reading past existing entries
	_, _, err = idx.Read(int64(len(entries)))
	require.Equal(t, io.EOF, err)
	_ = idx.Close()

	// index should build its state from the existing file
	f, _ = os.OpenFile(f.Name(), os.O_RDWR, 0600)
	idx, err = newIndex(f, c)
	require.NoError(t, err)
	off, pos, err := idx.Read(-1)
	require.NoError(t, err)
	require.Equal(t, uint32(1), off)
	require.Equal(t, entries[1].Pos, pos)
}
```

We iterate over each entry and write it to the index. We check that we can read the same entry back via the Read() method. Then we verify that the index and scanner error when we try to read beyond the number of entries stored in the index. And we check that the index builds its state from the existing file, for when our service restarts with existing data.

We need to configure the max size of a segment's store and index. Let's add a config struct to centralize the log's configuration, making it easy to configure the log and use the configs throughout the code. Create an internal/log/config.go file with the following code:

WriteALogPackage/internal/log/config.go

```
package log

type Config struct {
	Segment struct {
		MaxStoreBytes uint64
		MaxIndexBytes uint64
		InitialOffset uint64
	}
}
```

That wraps up the code for store and index types, which make up the lowest level of our log. Now let's code the segment.

Create the Segment

The segment wraps the index and store types to coordinate operations across the two. For example, when the log appends a record to the active segment, the segment needs to write the data to its store and add a new entry in the index. Similarly for reads, the segment needs to look up the entry from the index and then fetch the data from the store.

To get started, create a file called segment.go in internal/log that starts with the following code:

WriteALogPackage/internal/log/segment.go

```
package log

import (
	"fmt"
	"os"
	"path"

	api "github.com/travisjeffery/proglog/api/v1"
	"google.golang.org/protobuf/proto"
)

type segment struct {
	store                  *store
	index                  *index
	baseOffset, nextOffset uint64
	config                 Config
}
```

Our segment needs to call its store and index files, so we keep pointers to those in the first two fields. We need the next and base offsets to know what offset to append new records under and to calculate the relative offsets for the index entries. And we put the config on the segment so we can compare the store file and index sizes to the configured limits, which lets us know when the segment is maxed out.

Below the previous snippet, add the following newSegment() function:

WriteALogPackage/internal/log/segment.go

```
func newSegment(dir string, baseOffset uint64, c Config) (*segment, error) {
	s := &segment{
		baseOffset: baseOffset,
		config:     c,
	}
	var err error
	storeFile, err := os.OpenFile(
		path.Join(dir, fmt.Sprintf("%d%s", baseOffset, ".store")),
		os.O_RDWR|os.O_CREATE|os.O_APPEND,
		0644,
	)
	if err != nil {
		return nil, err
	}
	if s.store, err = newStore(storeFile); err != nil {
		return nil, err
	}
	indexFile, err := os.OpenFile(
		path.Join(dir, fmt.Sprintf("%d%s", baseOffset, ".index")),
		os.O_RDWR|os.O_CREATE,
		0644,
	)
	if err != nil {
		return nil, err
	}
	if s.index, err = newIndex(indexFile, c); err != nil {
		return nil, err
	}
	if off, _, err := s.index.Read(-1); err != nil {
		s.nextOffset = baseOffset
	} else {
		s.nextOffset = baseOffset + uint64(off) + 1
	}
	return s, nil
}
```

The log calls newSegment() when it needs to add a new segment, such as when the current active segment hits its max size. We open the store and index files and pass the os.O_CREATE file mode flag as an argument to os.OpenFile() to create the files if they don't exist yet. When we create the store file, we pass the os.O_APPEND flag to make the operating system append to the file when writing. Then we create our index and store with these files. Finally, we set the segment's next offset to prepare for the next appended record. If the index is empty, then the next record appended to the segment would be the first record and its offset would be the segment's base offset. If the index has at least one entry, then that means the offset of the next record written should take the offset at the end of the segment, which we get by adding 1 to the base offset and relative offset. Our segment is ready to write to and read from the log—once we've written those methods!

Next, below newSegment() put the following Append() method:

WriteALogPackage/internal/log/segment.go

```
func (s *segment) Append(record *api.Record) (offset uint64, err error) {
	cur := s.nextOffset
	record.Offset = cur
	p, err := proto.Marshal(record)
	if err != nil {
		return 0, err
	}
	_, pos, err := s.store.Append(p)
	if err != nil {
		return 0, err
	}
	if err = s.index.Write(
		// index offsets are relative to base offset
		uint32(s.nextOffset-uint64(s.baseOffset)),
		pos,
	); err != nil {
		return 0, err
	}
	s.nextOffset++
	return cur, nil
}
```

Append() writes the record to the segment and returns the newly appended record's offset. The log returns the offset to the API response. The segment appends a record in a two-step process: it appends the data to the store and then adds an index entry. Since index offsets are relative to the base offset, we subtract the segment's next offset from its base offset (which are both absolute offsets) to get the entry's relative offset in the segment. We then increment the next offset to prep for a future append call.

Now add the following Read() method below Append():

WriteALogPackage/internal/log/segment.go

```
func (s *segment) Read(off uint64) (*api.Record, error) {
	_, pos, err := s.index.Read(int64(off - s.baseOffset))
	if err != nil {
		return nil, err
	}
	p, err := s.store.Read(pos)
```

```
	if err != nil {
		return nil, err
	}
	record := &api.Record{}
	err = proto.Unmarshal(p, record)
	return record, err
}
```

Read(off uint64) returns the record for the given offset. Similar to writes, to read a record the segment must first translate the absolute index into a relative offset and get the associated index entry. Once it has the index entry, the segment can go straight to the record's position in the store and read the proper amount of data.

Next, put the following IsMaxed() method below Read():

WriteALogPackage/internal/log/segment.go

```
func (s *segment) IsMaxed() bool {
	return s.store.size >= s.config.Segment.MaxStoreBytes ||
		s.index.size >= s.config.Segment.MaxIndexBytes
}
```

IsMaxed() returns whether the segment has reached its max size, either by writing too much to the store or the index. If you wrote a small number of long logs, then you'd hit the segment bytes limit; if you wrote a lot of small logs, then you'd hit the index bytes limit. The log uses this method to know it needs to create a new segment.

Write this Remove() method below IsMaxed():

WriteALogPackage/internal/log/segment.go

```
func (s *segment) Remove() error {
	if err := s.Close(); err != nil {
		return err
	}
	if err := os.Remove(s.index.Name()); err != nil {
		return err
	}
	if err := os.Remove(s.store.Name()); err != nil {
		return err
	}
	return nil
}
```

Remove() closes the segment and removes the index and store files.

And put this Close() method below Remove():

WriteALogPackage/internal/log/segment.go

```
func (s *segment) Close() error {
	if err := s.index.Close(); err != nil {
		return err
	}
	if err := s.store.Close(); err != nil {
		return err
	}
	return nil
}
```

Finally, add this last function at the end of the file:

WriteALogPackage/internal/log/segment.go

```
func nearestMultiple(j, k uint64) uint64 {
	if j >= 0 {
		return (j / k) * k
	}
	return ((j - k + 1) / k) * k

}
```

nearestMultiple(j uint64, k uint64) returns the nearest and lesser multiple of k in j, for example nearestMultiple(9, 4) == 8. We take the lesser multiple to make sure we stay under the user's disk capacity.

That's all the segment code, so now let's test it. Create a segment_test.go file inside internal/log with the following test code:

WriteALogPackage/internal/log/segment_test.go

```
package log

import (
	"io"
	"io/ioutil"
	"os"
	"testing"

	"github.com/stretchr/testify/require"
	api "github.com/travisjeffery/proglog/api/v1"
)

func TestSegment(t *testing.T) {
	dir, _ := ioutil.TempDir("", "segment-test")
	defer os.RemoveAll(dir)

	want := &api.Record{Value: []byte("hello world")}

	c := Config{}
	c.Segment.MaxStoreBytes = 1024
	c.Segment.MaxIndexBytes = entWidth * 3

	s, err := newSegment(dir, 16, c)
	require.NoError(t, err)
```

```
	require.Equal(t, uint64(16), s.nextOffset, s.nextOffset)
	require.False(t, s.IsMaxed())

	for i := uint64(0); i < 3; i++ {
		off, err := s.Append(want)
		require.NoError(t, err)
		require.Equal(t, 16+i, off)

		got, err := s.Read(off)
		require.NoError(t, err)
		require.Equal(t, want.Value, got.Value)
	}

	_, err = s.Append(want)
	require.Equal(t, io.EOF, err)

	// maxed index
	require.True(t, s.IsMaxed())

	c.Segment.MaxStoreBytes = uint64(len(want.Value) * 3)
	c.Segment.MaxIndexBytes = 1024

	s, err = newSegment(dir, 16, c)
	require.NoError(t, err)
	// maxed store
	require.True(t, s.IsMaxed())

	err = s.Remove()
	require.NoError(t, err)
	s, err = newSegment(dir, 16, c)
	require.NoError(t, err)
	require.False(t, s.IsMaxed())
}
```

We test that we can append a record to a segment, read back the same record, and eventually hit the configured max size for both the store and index. Calling newSegment() twice with the same base offset and dir also checks that the function loads a segment's state from the persisted index and log files.

Now that we know that our segment works, we're ready to create the log.

Code the Log

All right, one last piece to go and that's the log, which manages the list of segments. Create a log.go file inside internal/log that starts with the following code:

WriteALogPackage/internal/log/log.go

```
package log

import (
	"fmt"
	"io"
	"io/ioutil"
	"os"
```

```
	"path"
	"sort"
	"strconv"
	"strings"
	"sync"

	api "github.com/travisjeffery/proglog/api/v1"
)

type Log struct {
	mu sync.RWMutex

	Dir    string
	Config Config

	activeSegment *segment
	segments      []*segment
}
```

The log consists of a list of segments and a pointer to the active segment to append writes to. The directory is where we store the segments.

Below the Log struct, write the following NewLog() function:

WriteALogPackage/internal/log/log.go

```
func NewLog(dir string, c Config) (*Log, error) {
	if c.Segment.MaxStoreBytes == 0 {
		c.Segment.MaxStoreBytes = 1024
	}
	if c.Segment.MaxIndexBytes == 0 {
		c.Segment.MaxIndexBytes = 1024
	}
	l := &Log{
		Dir:    dir,
		Config: c,
	}

	return l, l.setup()
}
```

In NewLog(dir string, c Config), we first set defaults for the configs the caller didn't specify, create a log instance, and set up that instance.

Next, add this setup() method below NewLog():

WriteALogPackage/internal/log/log.go

```
func (l *Log) setup() error {
	files, err := ioutil.ReadDir(l.Dir)
	if err != nil {
		return err
	}
	var baseOffsets []uint64
	for _, file := range files {
		offStr := strings.TrimSuffix(
```

```
				file.Name(),
				path.Ext(file.Name()),
			)
			off, _ := strconv.ParseUint(offStr, 10, 0)
			baseOffsets = append(baseOffsets, off)
	}
	sort.Slice(baseOffsets, func(i, j int) bool {
		return baseOffsets[i] < baseOffsets[j]
	})
	for i := 0; i < len(baseOffsets); i++ {
		if err = l.newSegment(baseOffsets[i]); err != nil {
			return err
		}
		// baseOffset contains dup for index and store so we skip
		// the dup
		i++
	}
	if l.segments == nil {
		if err = l.newSegment(
			l.Config.Segment.InitialOffset,
		); err != nil {
			return err
		}
	}
	return nil
}
```

When a log starts, it's responsible for setting itself up for the segments that already exist on disk or, if the log is new and has no existing segments, for bootstrapping the initial segment. We fetch the list of the segments on disk, parse and sort the base offsets (because we want our slice of segments to be in order from oldest to newest), and then create the segments with the newSegment() helper method, which creates a segment for the base offset you pass in.

Now add the following Append() function below setup():

WriteALogPackage/internal/log/log.go

```
func (l *Log) Append(record *api.Record) (uint64, error) {
	l.mu.Lock()
	defer l.mu.Unlock()
	off, err := l.activeSegment.Append(record)
	if err != nil {
		return 0, err
	}
	if l.activeSegment.IsMaxed() {
		err = l.newSegment(off + 1)
	}
	return off, err
}
```

Append(*api.Record) appends a record to the log. We append the record to the active segment. Afterward, if the segment is at its max size (per the max size configs), then we make a new active segment. Note that we're wrapping this func (and subsequent funcs) with a mutex to coordinate access to this section of the code. We use a RWMutex to grant access to reads when there isn't a write holding the lock. If you felt so inclined, you could optimize this further and make the locks per segment rather than across the whole log. (I haven't done that here because I want to keep this code simple.)

Below Append(), add this Read() method:

WriteALogPackage/internal/log/log.go

```
func (l *Log) Read(off uint64) (*api.Record, error) {
	l.mu.RLock()
	defer l.mu.RUnlock()
	var s *segment
	for _, segment := range l.segments {
		if segment.baseOffset <= off && off < segment.nextOffset {
			s = segment
			break
		}
	}
	if s == nil || s.nextOffset <= off {
		return nil, fmt.Errorf("offset out of range: %d", off)
	}
	return s.Read(off)
}
```

Read(offset uint64) reads the record stored at the given offset. In Read(offset uint64), we first find the segment that contains the given record. Since the segments are in order from oldest to newest and the segment's base offset is the smallest offset in the segment, we iterate over the segments until we find the first segment whose base offset is less than or equal to the offset we're looking for. Once we know the segment that contains the record, we get the index entry from the segment's index, and we read the data out of the segment's store file and return the data to the caller.

Below Read(), add this snippet to define the Close(), Remove(), and Reset() methods:

WriteALogPackage/internal/log/log.go

```
func (l *Log) Close() error {
	l.mu.Lock()
	defer l.mu.Unlock()
	for _, segment := range l.segments {
		if err := segment.Close(); err != nil {
			return err
		}
	}
```

```
	return nil
}

func (l *Log) Remove() error {
	if err := l.Close(); err != nil {
		return err
	}
	return os.RemoveAll(l.Dir)
}

func (l *Log) Reset() error {
	if err := l.Remove(); err != nil {
		return err
	}
	return l.setup()
}
```

This snippet implements a few related methods:

- Close() iterates over the segments and closes them.
- Remove() closes the log and then removes its data.
- Reset() removes the log and then creates a new log to replace it.

After the previous snippet, add this snippet to implement the LowestOffset() and HighestOffset() methods:

WriteALogPackage/internal/log/log.go

```
func (l *Log) LowestOffset() (uint64, error) {
	l.mu.RLock()
	defer l.mu.RUnlock()
	return l.segments[0].baseOffset, nil
}

func (l *Log) HighestOffset() (uint64, error) {
	l.mu.RLock()
	defer l.mu.RUnlock()
	off := l.segments[len(l.segments)-1].nextOffset
	if off == 0 {
		return 0, nil
	}
	return off - 1, nil
}
```

These methods tell us the offset range stored in the log. In Chapter 8, Coordinate Your Services with Consensus, on page 141, when we work on supporting a replicated, coordinated cluster, we'll need this information to know what nodes have the oldest and newest data and what nodes are falling behind and need to replicate.

Below HighestOffset(), add this Truncate() method:

WriteALogPackage/internal/log/log.go

```
func (l *Log) Truncate(lowest uint64) error {
	l.mu.Lock()
	defer l.mu.Unlock()
	var segments []*segment
	for _, s := range l.segments {
		if s.nextOffset <= lowest+1 {
			if err := s.Remove(); err != nil {
				return err
			}
			continue
		}
		segments = append(segments, s)
	}
	l.segments = segments
	return nil
}
```

Truncate(lowest uint64) removes all segments whose highest offset is lower than lowest. Because we don't have disks with infinite space, we'll periodically call Truncate() to remove old segments whose data we (hopefully) have processed by then and don't need anymore.

After Truncate(), add this snippet:

WriteALogPackage/internal/log/log.go

```
func (l *Log) Reader() io.Reader {
	l.mu.RLock()
	defer l.mu.RUnlock()
	readers := make([]io.Reader, len(l.segments))
	for i, segment := range l.segments {
		readers[i] = &originReader{segment.store, 0}
	}
	return io.MultiReader(readers...)
}

type originReader struct {
	*store
	off int64
}

func (o *originReader) Read(p []byte) (int, error) {
	n, err := o.ReadAt(p, o.off)
	o.off += int64(n)
	return n, err
}
```

Reader() returns an io.Reader to read the whole log. We'll need this capability when we implement coordinate consensus and need to support snapshots and restoring a log. Reader() uses an io.MultiReader() call to concatenate the segments' stores. The segment stores are wrapped by the originReader type for two reasons. The first reason is to satisfy the io.Reader interface so we can pass it into the io.MultiReader() call. The second is to ensure that we begin reading from the origin of the store and read its entire file.

We've got one last method to add to our log, and that's the function to create new segments. Copy the following newSegment() method below Read():

WriteALogPackage/internal/log/log.go

```
func (l *Log) newSegment(off uint64) error {
	s, err := newSegment(l.Dir, off, l.Config)
	if err != nil {
		return err
	}
	l.segments = append(l.segments, s)
	l.activeSegment = s
	return nil
}
```

newSegment(off int64) creates a new segment, appends that segment to the log's slice of segments, and makes the new segment the active segment so that subsequent append calls write to it.

You know the deal: it's time to test our log. Create a log_test.go inside internal/log that starts with the following code:

WriteALogPackage/internal/log/log_test.go

```
package log

import (
	"io/ioutil"
	"os"
	"testing"

	"github.com/stretchr/testify/require"
	api "github.com/travisjeffery/proglog/api/v1"
	"google.golang.org/protobuf/proto"
)

func TestLog(t *testing.T) {
	for scenario, fn := range map[string]func(
		t *testing.T, log *Log,
	){
		"append and read a record succeeds": testAppendRead,
		"offset out of range error":         testOutOfRangeErr,
		"init with existing segments":       testInitExisting,
		"reader":                            testReader,
		"truncate":                          testTruncate,
	} {
		t.Run(scenario, func(t *testing.T) {
			dir, err := ioutil.TempDir("", "store-test")
			require.NoError(t, err)
			defer os.RemoveAll(dir)
```

```
                        c := Config{}
                        c.Segment.MaxStoreBytes = 32
                        log, err := NewLog(dir, c)
                        require.NoError(t, err)

                        fn(t, log)
                })
        }
}
```

TestLog(*testing.T) defines a table of tests to, well, test the log. I used a table to write the log tests so we don't have to repeat the code that creates a new log for every test case.

Now, let's define the test cases. Put the following test cases below the TestLog() function:

WriteALogPackage/internal/log/log_test.go

```
func testAppendRead(t *testing.T, log *Log) {
        append := &api.Record{
                Value: []byte("hello world"),
        }
        off, err := log.Append(append)
        require.NoError(t, err)
        require.Equal(t, uint64(0), off)

        read, err := log.Read(off)
        require.NoError(t, err)
        require.Equal(t, append.Value, read.Value)
}
```

testAppendRead(*testing.T, *log.Log) tests that we can successfully append to and read from the log. When we append a record to the log, the log returns the offset it associated that record with. So, when we ask the log for the record at that offset, we expect to get the same record that we appended.

WriteALogPackage/internal/log/log_test.go

```
func testOutOfRangeErr(t *testing.T, log *Log) {
        read, err := log.Read(1)
        require.Nil(t, read)
        require.Error(t, err)
}
```

testOutOfRangeErr(*testing.T, *log.Log) tests that the log returns an error when we try to read an offset that's outside of the range of offsets the log has stored.

WriteALogPackage/internal/log/log_test.go

```
func testInitExisting(t *testing.T, o *Log) {
        append := &api.Record{
                Value: []byte("hello world"),
        }
```

```
	for i := 0; i < 3; i++ {
		_, err := o.Append(append)
		require.NoError(t, err)
	}
	require.NoError(t, o.Close())

	off, err := o.LowestOffset()
	require.NoError(t, err)
	require.Equal(t, uint64(0), off)
	off, err = o.HighestOffset()
	require.NoError(t, err)
	require.Equal(t, uint64(2), off)

	n, err := NewLog(o.Dir, o.Config)
	require.NoError(t, err)

	off, err = n.LowestOffset()
	require.NoError(t, err)
	require.Equal(t, uint64(0), off)
	off, err = n.HighestOffset()
	require.NoError(t, err)
	require.Equal(t, uint64(2), off)
}
```

testInitExisting(*testing.T, *log.Log) tests that when we create a log, the log bootstraps itself from the data stored by prior log instances. We append three records to the original log before closing it. Then we create a new log configured with the same directory as the old log. Finally, we confirm that the new log set itself up from the data stored by the original log.

WriteALogPackage/internal/log/log_test.go

```
func testReader(t *testing.T, log *Log) {
	append := &api.Record{
		Value: []byte("hello world"),
	}
	off, err := log.Append(append)
	require.NoError(t, err)
	require.Equal(t, uint64(0), off)

	reader := log.Reader()
	b, err := ioutil.ReadAll(reader)
	require.NoError(t, err)

	read := &api.Record{}
	err = proto.Unmarshal(b[lenWidth:], read)
	require.NoError(t, err)
	require.Equal(t, append.Value, read.Value)
}
```

testReader(*testing.T, *log.Log) tests that we can read the full, raw log as it's stored on disk so that we can snapshot and restore the logs in Finite-State Machine, on page 151.

WriteALogPackage/internal/log/log_test.go

```
func testTruncate(t *testing.T, log *Log) {
	append := &api.Record{
		Value: []byte("hello world"),
	}
	for i := 0; i < 3; i++ {
		_, err := log.Append(append)
		require.NoError(t, err)
	}

	err := log.Truncate(1)
	require.NoError(t, err)

	_, err = log.Read(0)
	require.Error(t, err)
}
```

testTruncate(*testing.T, *log.Log) tests that we can truncate the log and remove old segments that we don't need any more.

That wraps up our log code! We just wrote a log that's not *that* watered down from the log that drives Kafka, and we didn't even have to work too hard.

What You Learned

You now know what logs are, why they're important, and how they're used in various applications including distributed services. And then you learned how to build one! This log serves as the foundation of our distributed log. Now we can build a service on our library and make the library's functionality accessible to people on other computers.

Part II

Network

CHAPTER 4

Serve Requests with gRPC

We've set up our project and protocol buffers and written our log library. Currently, our library can only be used on a single computer by a single person at a time. Plus that person has to learn our library's API, run our code, and store the log on their disk—none of which most people will do, which limits our user base. We can solve these problems and appeal to a larger audience by turning our library into a web service. Compared to a program that runs on a single computer, networked services provide three major advantages:

- You can run them across multiple computers for availability and scalability.
- They allow multiple people to interact with the same data.
- They provide accessible interfaces that are easy for people to use.

Some situations where you'll want to write services to reap these advantages include providing a public API for your front end to hit, building internal infrastructure tools, and making a service to build your own business on (people rarely pay to use libraries).

In this chapter, we'll build on our library and make a service that allows multiple people to interact with the same data and runs across multiple computers. We won't add support for clusters right now; we'll do that in Chapter 8, Coordinate Your Services with Consensus, on page 141. The best tool I've found for serving requests across distributed services is Google's gRPC.

What Is gRPC?

When I was building distributed services in the past, the two common problems that drove me batty were maintaining compatibility and maintaining performance between clients and the server.

I wanted to ensure that clients and the server were always compatible—that the client was sending requests that the server understood, and vice versa with the server's responses. When I made breaking changes to the server, I wanted to ensure that old clients continued to work, and I accomplished this by versioning my API.

For maintaining good performance, your main priorities are optimizing your database queries and optimizing the algorithms you've used to implement your business logic. Once you've optimized those though, performance will often come down to how fast your service unmarshals requests and marshals responses, and down to reducing the overhead each time clients and the server communicate—like using a single, long-lasting connection rather than a new connection for each request.

So I was happy when Google released gRPC, an open source, high-performance RPC (remote procedure call) framework. gRPC has been a great help in solving these problems when building distributed systems, and I think you'll find that it simplifies your work. How does gRPC help you build services?

Goals When Building a Service

Here are the most important goals to aim for when you're building a networked service—and some info about how gRPC helps you achieve them:

Simplicity

Networked communication is technical and complex. When building our service, we want to focus on the problem it solves rather than the technical minutiae of request-response serialization, and so on. You want to work with APIs that abstract these details away. However, when you need to work at lower levels of abstraction, then you need those levels to be accessible.

On the spectrum of low- to high-level frameworks, in terms of the abstractions you're working with, gRPC is mid-to-high level. It's above a framework like Express since gRPC decides how to serialize and structure your endpoints and provides features like bidirectional streaming, but below a framework like Rails since Rails handles everything from handling requests to storing your data and structuring your application. gRPC is extendable via middleware, and its active community[1] has written middleware[2] to

1. https://github.com/grpc-ecosystem
2. https://github.com/grpc-ecosystem/go-grpc-middleware

solve a lot of the problems you'll face when building services—for example, logging, authentication, rate limiting, and tracing.

Maintainability

Writing the *first* version of a service is a brief period of the total time you'll spend working on the service. Once your service is live and people depend on it, you must maintain backward compatibility. With request-response type APIs, the simplest way to maintain backward compatibility is to version and run multiple instances of your API.

With gRPC, you can easily write and run separate versions of your services when you have major API changes, while still taking advantage of protobuf's field versioning for small changes. Having all your requests and responses type checked helps prevent accidentally introducing backward-*incompatible* changes as you and your peers build your service.

Security

When you expose a service on a network, you expose the service to whoever is on that network—potentially the whole Internet. It's important that you control who has access to your service and what they can do.

gRPC supports Secure Sockets Layer/Transport Layer Security (SSL/TLS) to encrypt all data exchanged between the client and server and lets you attach credentials to requests so you know which user is making each request. We'll discuss security in the next chapter.

Ease of use

The whole point of writing a service is to have people use it and solve some problem of theirs. The easier your service is to use, the more popular it will be. You go a long way toward making your service easy to use by telling your users when they're doing something wrong, such as calling your API with a bad request.

With gRPC, everything from your service methods to your requests and responses and their bodies are all defined in types. The compiler copies the comments from your protobuf to your code to help users when the type definitions aren't good enough. Your users will know whether they're using the API correctly thanks to their code being type checked. Having everything—requests, responses, models, and serialization—type checked is a big help to people learning how to use your service. gRPC also lets users look up the API's details with godoc. Many frameworks don't offer either of these handy features.

Performance

You want your service to be as fast as possible while using as few resources as possible. For example, if you can run your application on an n1-standard-1 (~$35 per month) instance on Google Cloud Platform rather than on an n1-standard-2 (~$71 per month) instance, that cuts your costs in half.

gRPC is built on solid foundations with protobuf and HTTP/2 because protobuf performs very well at serialization and HTTP/2 provides a means for long-lasting connections, which gRPC takes advantage of. So your service runs efficiently and doesn't cause unnecessarily high server bills.

Scalability

Scalability can refer to scaling up with load balancing to balance the load across multiple computers and to scaling up the number of people developing a project. gRPC helps make both types of scaling easier.

You can use different kinds of load balancing with gRPC[3] based on your needs, including thick client-side load balancing, proxy load balancing, look-aside load balancing, or service mesh.

For scaling up the number of people working on your project, gRPC lets you compile your service into clients and servers in the languages that gRPC supports. This allows people to use their own languages to build services that communicate with each other.

We now know what we want out of building our service, so let's create a gRPC service that fulfills our goals.

Define a gRPC Service

A gRPC service is essentially a group of related RPC endpoints—exactly how they're related is up to you. A common example is a RESTful grouping where the relation is that the endpoints operate on the same resource, but the grouping could be looser than that. In general, it's just a group of endpoints needed to solve some problem. In our case, the goal is to enable people to write to and read from their log.

Creating a gRPC service involves defining it in protobuf and then compiling your protocol buffers into code comprising the client and server stubs that you then implement. To get started, open log.proto, the file where we defined our Record message, and add the following service definition above those messages:

3. https://grpc.io/blog/grpc-load-balancing

ServeRequestsWithgRPC/api/v1/log.proto
```
service Log {
  rpc Produce(ProduceRequest) returns (ProduceResponse) {}
  rpc Consume(ConsumeRequest) returns (ConsumeResponse) {}
  rpc ConsumeStream(ConsumeRequest) returns (stream ConsumeResponse) {}
  rpc ProduceStream(stream ProduceRequest) returns (stream ProduceResponse) {}
}
```

The service keyword says that this is a service for the compiler to generate, and each RPC line is an endpoint in that service, specifying the type of request and response the endpoint accepts. The requests and responses are messages that the compiler turns into Go structs, like the ones we saw in the previous chapter.

We have two streaming endpoints:

- ConsumeStream—a server-side streaming RPC where the client sends a request to the server and gets back a stream to read a sequence of messages.
- ProduceStream—a bidirectional streaming RPC where both the client and server send a sequence of messages using a read-write stream. The two streams operate independently, so the clients and servers can read and write in whatever order they like. For example, the server could wait to receive all of the client's requests before sending back its response. You'd order your calls this way if your server needed to process the requests in batches or aggregate a response over multiple requests. Alternatively, the server could send back a response for each request in lockstep. You'd order your calls this way if each request required its own corresponding response.

Below your service definition, add the following code to define our requests and responses:

ServeRequestsWithgRPC/api/v1/log.proto
```
message ProduceRequest  {
  Record record = 1;
}

message ProduceResponse  {
  uint64 offset = 1;
}

message ConsumeRequest {
  uint64 offset = 1;
}

message ConsumeResponse {
  Record record = 2;
}
```

The request includes the record to produce to the log, and the response sends back the record's offset, which is essentially the record's identifier. Similarly with consuming: the user specifies the offset of the logs they want to consume, and the server responds back with the specified record.

To generate the client- and server-side code with our Log service definition, we need to tell the protobuf compiler to use the gRPC plugin.

Compile with the gRPC Plugin

This task takes just a second. Install the gRPC package by running this command:

```
$ go get google.golang.org/grpc@v1.32.0
$ go get google.golang.org/grpc/cmd/protoc-gen-go-grpc@v1.0.0
```

Then open up your Makefile and update your compile target to match the following to enable the gRPC plugin and compile our gRPC service:

ServeRequestsWithgRPC/Makefile

```
compile:
	protoc api/v1/*.proto \
		--go_out=. \
		--go-grpc_out=. \
		--go_opt=paths=source_relative \
		--go-grpc_opt=paths=source_relative \
		--proto_path=.
```

Run $ make compile, and then open up the log_grpc.pb.go file in the api/v1 directory and check out the generated code. You'll see a working gRPC log client, and the compiler left the log service API for us to implement.

Implement a gRPC Server

Because the compiler generated a server stub, the job left for us is to write it. To implement a server, you need to build a struct whose methods match the service definition in your protobuf.

Create an internal/server directory tree in the root of your project by running mkdir -p internal/server. Internal packages are magical packages in Go that can only be imported by nearby code. For example, you can import code in /a/b/c/internal/d/e/f by code rooted by /a/b/c, but not code rooted by /a/b/g. In this directory, we'll implement our server in a file called server.go and a package named server. The first order of business is to define our server type and a factory function to create an instance of the server.

Here's the code we need to add to our server.go file:

ServeRequestsWithgRPC/internal/server/server.go

```
package server

import (
	"context"

	api "github.com/travisjeffery/proglog/api/v1"
	"google.golang.org/grpc"
)

type Config struct {
	CommitLog CommitLog
}

var _ api.LogServer = (*grpcServer)(nil)

type grpcServer struct {
	api.UnimplementedLogServer
	*Config
}
func newgrpcServer(config *Config) (srv *grpcServer, err error) {
	srv = &grpcServer{
		Config: config,
	}
	return srv, nil
}
```

To implement the API you saw in log_grpc.pb.go, we need to implement the Consume() and Produce() handlers. Our gRPC layer is thin because it defers to our log library, so to implement these methods, you call down to the library and handle any errors. Add the following code below your newgrpcServer function:

ServeRequestsWithgRPC/internal/server/server.go

```
func (s *grpcServer) Produce(ctx context.Context, req *api.ProduceRequest) (
	*api.ProduceResponse, error) {
	offset, err := s.CommitLog.Append(req.Record)
	if err != nil {
		return nil, err
	}
	return &api.ProduceResponse{Offset: offset}, nil
}

func (s *grpcServer) Consume(ctx context.Context, req *api.ConsumeRequest) (
	*api.ConsumeResponse, error) {
	record, err := s.CommitLog.Read(req.Offset)
	if err != nil {
		return nil, err
	}
	return &api.ConsumeResponse{Record: record}, nil
}
```

With this snippet, we've implemented the Produce(context.Context, *api.ProduceRequest) and Consume(context.Context, *api.ConsumeRequest) methods on our server. These methods handle the requests made by clients to produce and consume to the server's log. Now let's add the streaming APIs. Put the following code below the previous snippet:

ServeRequestsWithgRPC/internal/server/server.go

```
func (s *grpcServer) ProduceStream(
	stream api.Log_ProduceStreamServer,
) error {
	for {
		req, err := stream.Recv()
		if err != nil {
			return err
		}
		res, err := s.Produce(stream.Context(), req)
		if err != nil {
			return err
		}
		if err = stream.Send(res); err != nil {
			return err
		}
	}
}

func (s *grpcServer) ConsumeStream(
	req *api.ConsumeRequest,
	stream api.Log_ConsumeStreamServer,
) error {
	for {
		select {
		case <-stream.Context().Done():
			return nil
		default:
			res, err := s.Consume(stream.Context(), req)
			switch err.(type) {
			case nil:
			case api.ErrOffsetOutOfRange:
				continue
			default:
				return err
			}
			if err = stream.Send(res); err != nil {
				return err
			}
			req.Offset++
		}
	}
}
```

ProduceStream(api.Log_ProduceStreamServer) implements a bidirectional streaming RPC so the client can stream data into the server's log and the server can tell the client whether each request succeeded. ConsumeStream(*api.ConsumeRequest, api.Log_ConsumeStreamServer) implements a server-side streaming RPC so the client can tell the server where in the log to read records, and then the server will stream every record that follows—even records that aren't in the log yet! When the server reaches the end of the log, the server will wait until someone appends a record to the log and then continue streaming records to the client.

The code that makes up our gRPC service is short and simple, which is a sign that we have a clean separation between our networking code and log code. However, one reason our service's code is so short is because we have the most basic error handling ever: we just send the client whatever error our library returned.

If a client tried to consume a message but the request failed, the developer would want to know why. Could the server not find the message? Did the server fail unexpectedly? The server communicates this info with a status code. Also, end users need to know when the application fails, so the server should send back a human-readable version of the error for the client to show to the user.

Let's explore how to improve our service's error handling, shall we?

Error Handling in gRPC

Yet another nice feature of gRPC is how it handles errors. In the previous code, we return errors just like you'd see in code from the Go standard library. Even though this code is handling calls between people on different computers, you wouldn't know it—thanks to gRPC, which abstracts away the networking details. By default your errors will only have a string description, but you may want to include more information such as a status code or some other arbitrary data.

Go's gRPC implementation has an awesome status package[4] that you can use to build errors with status codes or whatever other data you want to include in your errors. To create an error with a status code, you create the error with the Error function from the status package and pass the relevant code from the codes package[5] that matches the type of error you have. Any status code you attach on the error here must be a code defined in the codes package—they're meant to be consistent across the languages gRPC supports.

4. https://godoc.org/google.golang.org/grpc/status
5. https://godoc.org/google.golang.org/grpc/codes

For example, if you couldn't find a record for some ID, then you'd use the NotFound code like this:

```
err := status.Error(codes.NotFound, "id was not found")
return nil, err
```

On the client side, you'd parse out the code from the error with the FromError function from the status package. Your goal is to have as few non-status errors as possible so you know why the errors happen and can handle them gracefully. The non-status errors that are OK are unforeseen, internal server errors. Here's how to use the FromError function to parse out a status from a gRPC error:

```
st, ok := status.FromError(err)
if !ok {
    // Error was not a status error
}
// Use st.Message() and st.Code()
```

When you want more than a status code (say you're trying to debug an error and want more details like logs or traces), then you can use the status package's WithDetails function, which allows you to attach any protobuf message you want to the error.

The errdetailspackage[6] provides some protobufs you'll likely find useful when building your service, including messages to use to handle bad requests, debug info, and localized messages.

Let's use the LocalizedMessage from the errdetails package to change the previous example to respond with an error message that's safe to return to the user. In the following code, we first create a new not-found status, then we create the localized message specifying the message and locale used. Next we attach the details to the status, and then finally convert and return the status as a Go error:

```
st := status.New(codes.NotFound, "id was not found")
d := &errdetails.LocalizedMessage{
    Locale: "en-US",
    Message: fmt.Sprintf(
        "We couldn't find a user with the email address: %s",
        id,
    ),
}
var err error
st, err = st.WithDetails(d)
```

6. https://godoc.org/google.golang.org/genproto/googleapis/rpc/errdetails

```
if err != nil {
    // If this errored, it will always error
    // here, so better panic so we can figure
    // out why than have this silently passing.
    panic(fmt.Sprintf("Unexpected error attaching metadata: %v", err))
}
return st.Err()
```

To extract these details on the client side, you need to convert the error back into a status, pull out the details via its `Details` method, and then convert the type of the details to match the type of the protobuf you set on the server, which in our case is `*errdetails.LocalizedMessage`.

The code to do that looks like this:

```
st := status.Convert(err)
for _, detail := range st.Details() {
    switch t := detail.(type) {
    case *errdetails.LocalizedMessage:
        // send t.Message back to the user
    }
}
```

Focusing back on our service, let's add a custom error named `ErrOffsetOutOfRange` that the server will send back to the client when the client tries to consume an offset that's outside of the log. Create an `error.go` file inside the `api/v1` directory with the following code:

ServeRequestsWithgRPC/api/v1/error.go

```
package log_v1

import (
	"fmt"

	"google.golang.org/genproto/googleapis/rpc/errdetails"
	"google.golang.org/grpc/status"
)

type ErrOffsetOutOfRange struct {
	Offset uint64
}

func (e ErrOffsetOutOfRange) GRPCStatus() *status.Status {
	st := status.New(
		404,
		fmt.Sprintf("offset out of range: %d", e.Offset),
	)
	msg := fmt.Sprintf(
		"The requested offset is outside the log's range: %d",
		e.Offset,
	)
```

```
d := &errdetails.LocalizedMessage{
                Locale:  "en-US",
                Message: msg,
        }
        std, err := st.WithDetails(d)
        if err != nil {
                return st
        }
        return std
}

func (e ErrOffsetOutOfRange) Error() string {
        return e.GRPCStatus().Err().Error()
}
```

Next, let's update your log to use this error. Find this section of the Read(offset uint64) method of your log in internal/log/log.go:

WriteALogPackage/internal/log/log.go

```
if s == nil || s.nextOffset <= off {
        return nil, fmt.Errorf("offset out of range: %d", off)
}
```

And then change that section to this:

ServeRequestsWithgRPC/internal/log/log.go

```
if s == nil || s.nextOffset <= off {
        return nil, api.ErrOffsetOutOfRange{Offset: off}
}
```

Finally, we need to update the associated testOutOfRange(*testing.T, *log.Log) test in internal/log/log_test.go to the following code:

ServeRequestsWithgRPC/internal/log/log_test.go

```
func testOutOfRangeErr(t *testing.T, log *Log) {
        read, err := log.Read(1)
        require.Nil(t, read)
        apiErr := err.(api.ErrOffsetOutOfRange)
        require.Equal(t, uint64(1), apiErr.Offset)
}
```

With our custom error, when the client tries to consume an offset that's outside of the log, the log returns an error with plenty of useful information: a localized message, a status code, and an error message. Because our error is a struct type, we can type-switch the error returned by the Read(offset uint64) method to know what happened. We already use this feature in our ConsumeStream(*api.ConsumeRequest, api.Log_ConsumeStreamServer) method to know whether the server has read to the end of the log and just needs to wait until someone produces another record to the client:

ServeRequestsWithgRPC/internal/server/server.go

```
func (s *grpcServer) ConsumeStream(
	req *api.ConsumeRequest,
	stream api.Log_ConsumeStreamServer,
) error {
	for {
		select {
		case <-stream.Context().Done():
			return nil
		default:
			res, err := s.Consume(stream.Context(), req)
			switch err.(type) {
			case nil:
			case api.ErrOffsetOutOfRange:
				continue
			default:
				return err
			}
			if err = stream.Send(res); err != nil {
				return err
			}
			req.Offset++
		}
	}
}
```

We've improved our service's error handling to include status codes and a human-readable, localized error message to help our users know why a failure occurred. Next, let's define the log field that's on our service such that we can pass in different log implementations and make the service easier to write tests against.

Dependency Inversion with Interfaces

Our server depends on a log abstraction. For example, when running in a production environment—where we need our service to persist our user's data—the service will depend on our library. But when running in a test environment, where we *don't* need to persist our test data, we could use a naive, in-memory log. An in-memory log would also be good for testing because it would make the tests run faster.

As you can see from these examples, it would be best if our service weren't tied to a specific log implementation. Instead, we want to pass in a log implementation based on our needs at the time. We can make this possible by having our service depend on a log *interface* rather than on a concrete type. That way, the service can use any log implementation that satisfies the log interface.

Add this code below your grpcServer methods in server.go:

ServeRequestsWithgRPC/internal/server/server.go
```
type CommitLog interface {
	Append(*api.Record) (uint64, error)
	Read(uint64) (*api.Record, error)
}
```

That's all we need to do to allow our service to use *any* given log implementation that satisfies our CommitLog interface. Easy, huh?

Now, let's write an exported API that enables our users to instantiate a new service.

Register Your Server

We implemented the server writing nothing gRPC-specific yet. There are just three steps left to get our service working with gRPC, and happily we only need to perform two of them: creating a gRPC server and registering our service with it. The final step is giving the server a listener to accept incoming connections from, but we'll require our users to pass their own listener implementation, as they might like to when testing. Once these three steps are complete, the gRPC server will listen on the network, handle requests, call our server, and respond to the client with the result.

Above your grpcServer struct in server.go, add the following NewGRPCServer() function to provide your users a way to instantiate your service, create a gRPC server, and register your service to that server (this will give the user a server that just needs a listener for it to accept incoming connections):

ServeRequestsWithgRPC/internal/server/server.go
```
func NewGRPCServer(config *Config) (*grpc.Server, error) {
	gsrv := grpc.NewServer()
	srv, err := newgrpcServer(config)
	if err != nil {
		return nil, err
	}
	api.RegisterLogServer(gsrv, srv)
	return gsrv, nil
}
```

We're now done writing our service. Let's create some tests to verify that it works.

Test a gRPC Server and Client

Now that we've finished our gRPC server, we need some tests to check that our client and server work like we expect. We've already tested the details of our log's library implementation in the library, so the tests we're writing here are at a higher level and focus on ensuring that everything's hooked up properly between the gRPC and library bits and that our gRPC client and server can communicate.

In the grpc directory, create a server_test.go file, and add the following code that will set up your test:

ServeRequestsWithgRPC/internal/server/server_test.go

```
package server

import (
	"context"
	"io/ioutil"
	"net"
	"testing"

	"github.com/stretchr/testify/require"
	api "github.com/travisjeffery/proglog/api/v1"
	"github.com/travisjeffery/proglog/internal/log"
	"google.golang.org/grpc"
)

func TestServer(t *testing.T) {
	for scenario, fn := range map[string]func(
		t *testing.T,
		client api.LogClient,
		config *Config,
	){
		"produce/consume a message to/from the log succeeeds":
			testProduceConsume,
		"produce/consume stream succeeds":
			testProduceConsumeStream,
		"consume past log boundary fails":
			testConsumePastBoundary,
	} {
		t.Run(scenario, func(t *testing.T) {
			client, config, teardown := setupTest(t, nil)
			defer teardown()
			fn(t, client, config)
		})
	}
}
```

TestServer(*testing.T) defines our list of test cases and then runs a subtest for each case. Add the following setupTest(*testing.T, func(*Config)) function below TestServer():

ServeRequestsWithgRPC/internal/server/server_test.go

```
func setupTest(t *testing.T, fn func(*Config)) (
	client api.LogClient,
	cfg *Config,
	teardown func(),
) {
```

```
	t.Helper()

	l, err := net.Listen("tcp", ":0")
	require.NoError(t, err)

	clientOptions := []grpc.DialOption{grpc.WithInsecure()}
	cc, err := grpc.Dial(l.Addr().String(), clientOptions...)
	require.NoError(t, err)

	dir, err := ioutil.TempDir("", "server-test")
	require.NoError(t, err)

	clog, err := log.NewLog(dir, log.Config{})
	require.NoError(t, err)

	cfg = &Config{
		CommitLog: clog,
	}
	if fn != nil {
		fn(cfg)
	}
	server, err := NewGRPCServer(cfg)
	require.NoError(t, err)

	go func() {
		server.Serve(l)
	}()

	client = api.NewLogClient(cc)

	return client, cfg, func() {
		server.Stop()
		cc.Close()
		l.Close()
		clog.Remove()
	}
}
```

setupTest(*testing.T, func(*Config)) is a helper function to set up each test case. Our test setup begins by creating a listener on the local network address that our server will run on. The 0 port is useful for when we don't care what port we use since 0 will automatically assign us a free port. We then make an insecure connection to our listener and, with it, a client we'll use to hit our server with. Next we create our server and start serving requests in a goroutine because the Serve method is a blocking call, and if we didn't run it in a goroutine our tests further down would never run.

Now we're ready to write some test cases. Add the following code below setupTest():

ServeRequestsWithgRPC/internal/server/server_test.go

```
func testProduceConsume(t *testing.T, client api.LogClient, config *Config) {
	ctx := context.Background()
```

```
	want := &api.Record{
		Value: []byte("hello world"),
	}

	produce, err := client.Produce(
		ctx,
		&api.ProduceRequest{
			Record: want,
		},
	)
	require.NoError(t, err)

	consume, err := client.Consume(ctx, &api.ConsumeRequest{
		Offset: produce.Offset,
	})
	require.NoError(t, err)
	require.Equal(t, want.Value, consume.Record.Value)
	require.Equal(t, want.Offset, consume.Record.Offset)
}
```

testProduceConsume(*testing.T, api.LogClient, *Config) tests that producing and consuming works by using our client and server to produce a record to the log, consume it back, and then check that the record we sent is the same one we got back.

Add the following test case below testProduceConsume():

ServeRequestsWithgRPC/internal/server/server_test.go

```
func testConsumePastBoundary(
	t *testing.T,
	client api.LogClient,
	config *Config,
) {
	ctx := context.Background()

	produce, err := client.Produce(ctx, &api.ProduceRequest{
		Record: &api.Record{
			Value: []byte("hello world"),
		},
	})
	require.NoError(t, err)

	consume, err := client.Consume(ctx, &api.ConsumeRequest{
		Offset: produce.Offset + 1,
	})
	if consume != nil {
		t.Fatal("consume not nil")
	}
	got := grpc.Code(err)
	want := grpc.Code(api.ErrOffsetOutOfRange{}.GRPCStatus().Err())
	if got != want {
		t.Fatalf("got err: %v, want: %v", got, want)
	}
}
```

testConsumePastBoundary(*testing.T, api.LogClient, *Config) tests that our server responds with an api.ErrOffsetOutOfRange() error when a client tries to consume beyond the log's boundaries.

We have one more test case. Put the following snippet at the bottom of the file:

ServeRequestsWithgRPC/internal/server/server_test.go

```
func testProduceConsumeStream(
	t *testing.T,
	client api.LogClient,
	config *Config,
) {
	ctx := context.Background()

	records := []*api.Record{{
		Value:  []byte("first message"),
		Offset: 0,
	}, {
		Value:  []byte("second message"),
		Offset: 1,
	}}

	{
		stream, err := client.ProduceStream(ctx)
		require.NoError(t, err)

		for offset, record := range records {
			err = stream.Send(&api.ProduceRequest{
				Record: record,
			})
			require.NoError(t, err)
			res, err := stream.Recv()
			require.NoError(t, err)
			if res.Offset != uint64(offset) {
				t.Fatalf(
					"got offset: %d, want: %d",
					res.Offset,
					offset,
				)
			}
		}

	}

	{
		stream, err := client.ConsumeStream(
			ctx,
			&api.ConsumeRequest{Offset: 0},
		)
		require.NoError(t, err)

		for i, record := range records {
			res, err := stream.Recv()
```

```
                        require.NoError(t, err)
                        require.Equal(t, res.Record, &api.Record{
                                Value:  record.Value,
                                Offset: uint64(i),
                        })
                }
        }
}
```

testProduceConsumeStream(*testing.T, api.LogClient, *Config) is the streaming counterpart to testProduceConsume(), testing that we can produce and consume through streams.

Run $ make test to test your code. In the test output, you'll see your TestServer test passing.

Wahoo! You've written and tested your first gRPC service.

What You Learned

You now know how to define a gRPC service in protobuf, compile your gRPC protobufs into code, build a gRPC server, and test that everything works end-to-end across your client and server. You can build a gRPC server and client, and you can use your log over the network.

Next we'll improve the security of our service by encrypting the data sent between the client and server with SSL/TLS, and authenticating requests so we can know who's making each request and whether they're allowed to.

CHAPTER 5

Secure Your Services

When you build a project, your goal is to solve a problem. You may get so focused on this goal that you ignore the other factors you should consider, like security. Security is one of those things that's super important but easy to ignore.

Yes, creating a secure solution is more complicated than building a solution without considering security. But if you want to build something that people will actually use, it has to be secure. And it's far easier to incorporate security from the start than it is to retrofit security into a finished project. So you need to keep security in mind from the very beginning. In this book, for example, we don't just want to build a tool to stream data—we want to build a tool that streams data *securely*.

When you start your career as a software engineer, security can seem like a thankless job. If you do it right, no one will know you did it at all, and building it can be scary and even boring at times. Over the years, from building several software-as-a-service startups, I've changed my tune—I now consider securing my services as important as the problems they solve. Here's why:

- Security saves you from being hacked. When you don't follow security best practices, breaches and leaks follow with amazing regularity and severity, as we've seen in the news. Whenever I'm building a service, I think about what it'd be like if the data I'm trying to protect was publicly posted all over the planet. Picturing this gives me the motivation to make sure that sort of thing doesn't happen to me, and thankfully it hasn't yet (knock on wood).
- Security wins deals. In my experience, the most important factor in whether a potential customer bought software I worked on came down to whether the software fulfilled some security requirement.

- Security is painful to tack on. Taking an insecure service that lacks the basic security features most people need and then trying to tack those features on is a painful, tricky process. In contrast, it's relatively easy to build those features from the start.

Those high stakes get me fired up about building secure services. So let's get to it.

Secure Services in Three Steps

Security in distributed services can be broken down into three steps:

1. Encrypt data in-flight to protect against man-in-the-middle attacks;
2. Authenticate to identify clients; and
3. Authorize to determine the permissions of the identified clients.

Let's talk about these phases in more detail, explore the security benefits they provide, and write the code to build them into our service.

Encrypt In-Flight Data

Encryption of data in-flight prevents man-in-the-middle attacks (MITM).[1] An example of a MITM attack is active eavesdropping, where the attacker makes independent connections with the victims to make them think they're talking directly with each other when in fact the conversation is controlled by the attacker. This is bad because not only can the attacker learn confidential information, but also the attacker can maliciously change the messages sent between the victims. For example, say Bob was trying to send money to Alice using PayPal, but Mallory changed the account the money was sent to from Alice's to her own.

Cryptography's Conventional Names

Bob, Alice, and Mallory are placeholder names commonly used when discussing cryptography (en.wikipedia.org/wiki/Alice_and_Bob#Cast_of_characters). Typically Alice and Bob want to exchange a message, and Mallory is a malicious attacker. There's a whole cast of characters, and they're named with rhyming mnemonics to their role (for example: Mallory the malicious attacker, Eve the eavesdropper, Craig the password cracker).

The most widely used technology for preventing MITM attacks and encrypting data in-flight is TLS, the successor to SSL. TLS used to be considered necessary

1. https://en.wikipedia.org/wiki/Man-in-the-middle_attack

only for "serious" websites like online banks, but these days all sites should use TLS.[2] Modern browsers highlight websites that don't use TLS as unsafe and recommend their users to not even use them.

The process by which a client and server communicate is kicked off by a TLS handshake. During this handshake, the client and server:

1. Specify which version of TLS they'll use;
2. Decide which cipher suites (the set of encryption algorithms) they'll use;
3. Authenticate the identity of the server via the server's private key and the certificate authority's digital signature; and
4. Generate session keys for symmetric encryption after the handshake is complete.

Once this handshake process is complete, the client and server can communicate securely.

Fortunately we don't have to worry about implementing these TLS handshake steps, as TLS handles them for us behind the scenes. Our job is to obtain certificates for our client and server to use and to tell gRPC to communicate over TLS using the given the certs.

We'll build TLS support into our service to encrypt data in-flight and authenticate the server.

Authenticate to Identify Clients

Once you've secured the communication between your client and server with TLS, the next step to a secure service is authentication. Authentication is the process of identifying who the *client* is (TLS has already handled authenticating the server). For example, whenever you post a tweet, Twitter needs to verify that the person trying to post the tweet to your account is really you.

Most web services use TLS for one-way authentication and only authenticate the server. The authentication of the client is left to the application to work out, usually by some combination of username-password credentials and tokens. TLS mutual authentication, also commonly referred to as two-way authentication, in which both the server and the client validate the other's communication, is more commonly used in machine-to-machine communication—like distributed systems! In this setup, both the server and the client use a certificate to prove their identity.

2. https://doesmysiteneedhttps.com

Because mutual TLS authentication is so effective, relatively simple, and well adopted (both in terms of how many people use it and the number of technologies that support it), many companies use it to secure the communications[3] between their internal distributed services. Because so many people use mutual TLS authentication, it's important for new services (like ours) to support it. So we'll build mutual TLS authentication into our service.

Authorize to Determine the Permissions of Clients

Authentication and authorization are so closely related that people often use the word "auth" to refer to both. Authentication and authorization are almost always done at the same time in terms of the request's life-cycle and place in the server's code base. In fact, for many web services where resources have a single owner, authentication and authorization are the same process. For example, a Twitter account has one owner, so if a client authenticates as that owner, then Twitter lets them do whatever they want with the account.

Differentiating between authentication and authorization is necessary when you have a resource with shared access and varying levels of ownership. With our log service for example, Alice might be the owner and have both read and write access to the contents of the log, whereas Bob might be allowed to read the contents but isn't able to write. In this type of situation, you need authorization with granular access control.

In our service, we'll build access control list-based authorization to control whether a client is allowed to read from or write to (or both) the log.

Now that you have a general understanding of the three key aspects of securing a distributed system, let's implement them in our service.

Authenticate the Server with TLS

You've now seen how TLS works and why to use it, so we're ready to build TLS support into our service to encrypt data in-flight and authenticate the server. I'll also cover how to make obtaining and working with certificates easier to manage.

Operate as Your Own CA with CFSSL

Before changing our server's code, let's get some certs. We could use a third-party certificate authority (CA) to get the certs, but that could cost money (depending on the CA) and is a hassle. For internal services (like ours), there's

3. https://blog.cloudflare.com/how-to-build-your-own-public-key-infrastructure

no need to go through a third-party authority. Trusted certificates don't have to come from Comodo or Let's Encrypt or any other CA—they can come from a CA you operate yourself. It's free and easy with the right tools.

CloudFlare[4] wrote a toolkit called CFSSL for signing, verifying, and bundling TLS certificates. CloudFlare uses CFSSL for their internal services' TLS certificates, acting as their own certificate authority. CloudFlare open sourced CFSSL so others, including us, can use it. Even major CA vendors like Let's Encrypt use CFSSL. Big thanks to CloudFlare because CFSSL is a seriously useful toolkit.

CFSSL has two tools we'll need:

- cfssl to sign, verify, and bundle TLS certificates and output the results as JSON.
- cfssljson to take that JSON output and split them into separate key, certificate, CSR, and bundle files.

Install the CloudFlare CLIs by running the following commands:

```
$ go get github.com/cloudflare/cfssl/cmd/cfssl@v1.4.1
$ go get github.com/cloudflare/cfssl/cmd/cfssljson@v1.4.1
```

To initialize our CA and generate certs, we need to pass various config files to the cfssl commands we'll run. We need separate config files to generate our CA and server certs and we need a config file containing general config info about our CA. So let's create a directory in our project to contain these config files by running `$ mkdir test`.

Put the following JSON into a file called ca-csr.json in your test directory:

SecureYourServices/test/ca-csr.json

```
{
    "CN": "My Awesome CA",
    "key": {
        "algo": "rsa",
        "size": 2048
    },
    "names": [
        {
            "C": "CA",
            "L": "ON",
            "ST": "Toronto",
            "O": "My Awesome Company",
            "OU": "CA Services"
        }
    ]
}
```

4. https://www.cloudflare.com

cfssl will use this file to configure our CA's certificate. CN stands for *Common Name*, so we're saying our CA is called "My Awesome CA." key specifies the algorithm and size of key to sign the certificate with; names is a list of various name information that'll be added to the certificate. Each name object should contain at least one "C," "L," "O," "OU," or "ST" value (or any combination of these). They stand for:

- C—country
- L—locality or municipality (such as city)
- ST—state or province
- O—organization
- OU—organizational unit (such as the department responsible for owning the key)

Create a test/ca-config.json that looks like this to define the CA's policy:

SecureYourServices/test/ca-config.json

```
{
    "signing": {
        "profiles": {
            "server": {
                "expiry": "8760h",
                "usages": [
                    "signing",
                    "key encipherment",
                    "server auth"
                ]
            },
            "client": {
                "expiry": "8760h",
                "usages": [
                    "signing",
                    "key encipherment",
                    "client auth"
                ]
            }
        }
    }
}
```

Our CA needs to know what kind of certificates it will issue. The signing section of this configuration file defines your CA's signing policy. Our configuration file says that the CA can generate client and server certificates that will expire after a year and the certificates may be used for digital signatures, encrypting keys, and auth.

Put the following JSON into a file called server-csr.json in your test directory:

SecureYourServices/test/server-csr.json

```
{
    "CN": "127.0.0.1",
    "hosts": [
        "localhost",
        "127.0.0.1"
    ],
    "key": {
        "algo": "rsa",
        "size": 2048
    },
    "names": [
        {
            "C": "CA",
            "L": "ON",
            "ST": "Toronto",
            "O": "My Awesome Company",
            "OU": "Distributed Services"
        }
    ]
}
```

cfssl will use these configs to configure our server's certificate. The "hosts" field is a list of the domain names that the certificate should be valid for. Since we're running our service locally, we just need 127.0.0.1 and localhost.

Now let's update our Makefile to call cfssl and cfssljson to actually generate the certs. Make your project's Makefile look like this:

SecureYourServices/Makefile

```
CONFIG_PATH=${HOME}/.proglog/

.PHONY: init
init:
	mkdir -p ${CONFIG_PATH}

.PHONY: gencert
gencert:
	cfssl gencert \
		-initca test/ca-csr.json | cfssljson -bare ca

	cfssl gencert \
		-ca=ca.pem \
		-ca-key=ca-key.pem \
		-config=test/ca-config.json \
		-profile=server \
		test/server-csr.json | cfssljson -bare server
	mv *.pem *.csr ${CONFIG_PATH}

.PHONY: test
test:
	go test -race ./...
```

```
.PHONY: compile
compile:
	protoc api/v1/*.proto \
		--go_out=. \
		--go-grpc_out=. \
		--go_opt=paths=source_relative \
		--go-grpc_opt=paths=source_relative \
		--proto_path=.
```

In this updated Makefile, we've added a CONFIG_PATH variable to specify where we'd like to put our generated certs and an init target to create that directory. With these configs in a static and known location on the filesystem, it's easier to look up and use the certs in our code. The gencert target calls cfssl to generate the certificate and private keys for our CA and server using the config files we added earlier.

We'll reference these config files frequently in our tests, so let's make a package containing their file paths as variables to make referencing them easy. Create an internal/config directory with a files.go file containing this code:

SecureYourServices/internal/config/files.go

```go
package config

import (
	"os"
	"path/filepath"
)

var (
	CAFile               = configFile("ca.pem")
	ServerCertFile       = configFile("server.pem")
	ServerKeyFile        = configFile("server-key.pem")
)


func configFile(filename string) string {
	if dir := os.Getenv("CONFIG_DIR"); dir != "" {
		return filepath.Join(dir, filename)
	}
	homeDir, err := os.UserHomeDir()
	if err != nil {
		panic(err)
	}
	return filepath.Join(homeDir, ".proglog", filename)
}
```

These variables define the paths to the certs we generated and need to look up and parse for our tests. I would use constants and the const keyword if Go allowed using const with function calls.

We'll use the certificate and key files to build *tls.Configs, so let's add a helper function and struct for that. In the config directory, create a tls.go file beginning with this code:

SecureYourServices/internal/config/tls.go

```
package config

import (
	"crypto/tls"
	"crypto/x509"
	"fmt"
	"io/ioutil"
)

func SetupTLSConfig(cfg TLSConfig) (*tls.Config, error) {
	var err error
	tlsConfig := &tls.Config{}
	if cfg.CertFile != "" && cfg.KeyFile != "" {
		tlsConfig.Certificates = make([]tls.Certificate, 1)
		tlsConfig.Certificates[0], err = tls.LoadX509KeyPair(
			cfg.CertFile,
			cfg.KeyFile,
		)
		if err != nil {
			return nil, err
		}
	}
	if cfg.CAFile != "" {
		b, err := ioutil.ReadFile(cfg.CAFile)
		if err != nil {
			return nil, err
		}
		ca := x509.NewCertPool()
		ok := ca.AppendCertsFromPEM([]byte(b))
		if !ok {
			return nil, fmt.Errorf(
				"failed to parse root certificate: %q",
				cfg.CAFile,
			)
		}
		if cfg.Server {
			tlsConfig.ClientCAs = ca
			tlsConfig.ClientAuth = tls.RequireAndVerifyClientCert
		} else {
			tlsConfig.RootCAs = ca
		}
		tlsConfig.ServerName = cfg.ServerAddress
	}
	return tlsConfig, nil
}
```

Our tests use a few different *tls.Config configurations, and SetupTLSConfig() allows us to get each type of *tls.Config with one function call. These are the different configurations:

- Client *tls.Config is set up to verify the server's certificate with the client's by setting the *tls.Config's RootCAs.
- Client *tls.Config is set up to verify the server's certificate and allow the server to verify the client's certificate by setting its RootCAs and its Certificates.
- Server *tls.Config is set up to verify the client's certificate and allow the client to verify the server's certificate by setting its ClientCAs, Certificate, and ClientAuth mode set to tls.RequireAndVerifyCert.

Below SetupTLSConfig(), put this struct:

SecureYourServices/internal/config/tls.go
```
type TLSConfig struct {
        CertFile      string
        KeyFile       string
        CAFile        string
        ServerAddress string
        Server        bool
}
```

TLSConfig defines the parameters that SetupTLSConfig() uses to determine what type of *tls.Config to return.

Back to our tests. Let's test that the client uses our CA to verify the server's certificate. If the server's certificate came from a different authority, the client wouldn't trust the server and wouldn't make a connection. In setup_test.go, add these imports:

SecureYourServices/internal/server/server_test.go
```
"github.com/travisjeffery/proglog/internal/config"
"google.golang.org/grpc/credentials"
```

Now replace the code in your existing setupTest() function with the following code:

SecureYourServices/internal/server/server_test.go
```
t.Helper()

l, err := net.Listen("tcp", "127.0.0.1:0")
require.NoError(t, err)

clientTLSConfig, err := config.SetupTLSConfig(config.TLSConfig{
        CAFile: config.CAFile,
})
require.NoError(t, err)

clientCreds := credentials.NewTLS(clientTLSConfig)
cc, err := grpc.Dial(
```

```
        l.Addr().String(),
        grpc.WithTransportCredentials(clientCreds),
)
require.NoError(t, err)

client = api.NewLogClient(cc)
```

In this code, we configure our client's TLS credentials to use our CA as the client's Root CA (the CA it will use to verify the server). Then we tell the client to use those credentials for its connection.

Next we need to hook up our server with its certificate and enable it to handle TLS connections. Add the following code below the previous snippet:

SecureYourServices/internal/server/server_test.go

```
serverTLSConfig, err := config.SetupTLSConfig(config.TLSConfig{
        CertFile:      config.ServerCertFile,
        KeyFile:       config.ServerKeyFile,
        CAFile:        config.CAFile,
        ServerAddress: l.Addr().String(),
})
require.NoError(t, err)
serverCreds := credentials.NewTLS(serverTLSConfig)

dir, err := ioutil.TempDir("", "server-test")
require.NoError(t, err)

clog, err := log.NewLog(dir, log.Config{})
require.NoError(t, err)

cfg = &Config{
        CommitLog: clog,
}
if fn != nil {
        fn(cfg)
}
server, err := NewGRPCServer(cfg, grpc.Creds(serverCreds))
require.NoError(t, err)

go func() {
        server.Serve(l)
}()

return client, cfg, func() {
        server.Stop()
        cc.Close()
        l.Close()
}
```

In this code, we're parsing the server's cert and key, which we then use to configure the server's TLS credentials. We then pass those credentials as a gRPC server option to our NewGRPCServer() function so it can create our gRPC server with that option. gRPC server options are how you enable features in gRPC servers. We're setting the credentials for the server connections in this case, but there are plenty of other server options[5] to configure connection timeouts, keep alive policies, and so on.

Finally, we need to update the NewGRPCServer() function in server.go to take in the given gRPC server options and create the server with them. Change the NewGRPCServer() function to this:

SecureYourServices/internal/server/server.go

```
func NewGRPCServer(config *Config, opts ...grpc.ServerOption) (
	*grpc.Server,
	error,
) {
	gsrv := grpc.NewServer(opts...)
	srv, err := newgrpcServer(config)
	if err != nil {
		return nil, err
	}
	api.RegisterLogServer(gsrv, srv)
	return gsrv, nil
}
```

At this point you can run the tests with $ make test, and our tests should pass as they did before the changes we've made in this chapter. The difference is that your server is now authenticated and your connection is encrypted. You can verify this by temporarily changing your test code back to using an insecure client connection with the grpc.WithInsecure() dial option, and then running the tests again. This time the tests will fail because the client and server won't be able to connect with each other because the server is expecting the client to run over TLS.

Your server is authenticated so you know your client is communicating with your actual server and not some middleman's. Now we'll use mutual TLS authentication to verify that the client hitting your server really *is* your client.

Authenticate the Client with Mutual TLS Authentication

In the previous section, we used TLS to encrypt our connections and authenticate the server. Now we'll go one step further and implement mutual TLS authentication (also known as *two-way authentication*) so the server will use our CA to verify that the client is authentic.

The first thing we need is a cert for our client, which we can generate with cfssl and cfssljson just like our CA and server's certificates. Put the following JSON in a file called client-csr.json in your test directory:

---

5. https://godoc.org/google.golang.org/grpc#ServerOption

SecureYourServices/test/client-csr.json

```
{
    "CN": "client",
    "hosts": [""],
    "key": {
        "algo": "rsa",
        "size": 2048
    },
    "names": [
        {
            "C": "CA",
            "L": "ON",
            "ST": "Toronto",
            "O": "My Company",
            "OU": "Distributed Services"
        }
    ]
}
```

The CN field is the important config because that's the client's identity—their username, in a sense. This is the identity we'll store their permissions under for authorization. (We'll do this in the next section.)

Next, update the gencert target in your Makefile, to include the following snippet. Place it right below where you generate the server cert:

SecureYourServices/Makefile

```
cfssl gencert \
        -ca=ca.pem \
        -ca-key=ca-key.pem \
        -config=test/ca-config.json \
        -profile=client \
        test/client-csr.json | cfssljson -bare client
```

Once that is done, generate the cert for your client by running `$ make gencert`.

Add configuration file variables for your client certificates in internal/config/files.go:

SecureYourServices/internal/config/files.go

```
var (
        CAFile                = configFile("ca.pem")
        ServerCertFile        = configFile("server.pem")
        ServerKeyFile         = configFile("server-key.pem")
➤       ClientCertFile        = configFile("client.pem")
➤       ClientKeyFile         = configFile("client-key.pem")
)
```

Next we need to update the server to verify that the certificate the client has sent the server is signed by our CA. Update your server setup in server_test.go like this:

SecureYourServices/internal/server/server_test.go

```
clientTLSConfig, err := config.SetupTLSConfig(config.TLSConfig{
        CertFile: config.ClientCertFile,
        KeyFile:  config.ClientKeyFile,
        CAFile: config.CAFile,
})
require.NoError(t, err)

clientCreds := credentials.NewTLS(clientTLSConfig)
cc, err := grpc.Dial(
        l.Addr().String(),
        grpc.WithTransportCredentials(clientCreds),
)
require.NoError(t, err)

client = api.NewLogClient(cc)

serverTLSConfig, err := config.SetupTLSConfig(config.TLSConfig{
        CertFile:      config.ServerCertFile,
        KeyFile:       config.ServerKeyFile,
        CAFile:        config.CAFile,
        ServerAddress: l.Addr().String(),
        Server: true,
})
```

Now run your tests again. They'll still pass because you're using a valid cert and your tests expect the client to be authentic. For a fun exercise, try generating a cert from a different CA for your client to use and then watch your tests fail. (Okay, maybe I'm the only one who considers this kind of thing fun.)

Your server and client now have mutual TLS authentication with both sides verifying that your CA vouches for their authenticity, so you know it's your actual client communicating with your server without a middleman eavesdropping. Hooray for security!

Authorize with Access Control Lists

Authentication is usually half of what you need from your auth process. You *authenticate* to know who's behind the client so you can then complete the auth process by *authorizing* whoever is behind the client for whatever action they've attempted. As I mentioned earlier, authorization is the process of verifying what someone has access to.

The simplest way to implement authorization is with an access control list (ACL).[6] An ACL is a table of rules where each row says something like "Subject A is permitted to do action B on object C." For example: Alice is permitted to

6. https://en.wikipedia.org/wiki/Access_control_list

read *Distributed Services with Go*. In this example, Alice is the subject, to read is the action, and *Distributed Services with Go* is the object.

One of the beautiful things about an ACL is that it's easy to build. Since it's just a table, something as simple as a map or a CSV file could back the data—in more complex implementations, a key-value store or relational database would store the data. So building an ACL library from scratch isn't difficult, but there's a nice library called Casbin[7] that supports enforcing authorization based on various control models[8]—including ACLs. Plus Casbin is well adopted, tested, and extendable. Casbin is a useful tool to have in your toolkit, so let's learn how to use it and take advantage of it!

First, add Casbin as a dependency by running the following command at the root of your project:

```
$ go get github.com/casbin/casbin@v1.9.1
```

We'll wrap Casbin with our own internal library. If we later use another authorization tool, we won't have to change a bunch of code throughout our project, just the code in our library. Create an auth directory inside your internal directory by running:

```
$ mkdir internal/auth
```

Then create a file called authorizer.go in that directory with your favorite text editor and add the following code:

SecureYourServices/internal/auth/authorizer.go

```
package auth

import (
	"fmt"

	"github.com/casbin/casbin"
	"google.golang.org/grpc/codes"
	"google.golang.org/grpc/status"
)

func New(model, policy string) *Authorizer {
	enforcer := casbin.NewEnforcer(model, policy)
	return &Authorizer{
		enforcer: enforcer,
	}
}

type Authorizer struct {
	enforcer *casbin.Enforcer
}
```

7. https://github.com/casbin/casbin
8. https://github.com/casbin/casbin#supported-models

```
func (a *Authorizer) Authorize(subject, object, action string) error {
	if !a.enforcer.Enforce(subject, object, action) {
		msg := fmt.Sprintf(
			"%s not permitted to %s to %s",
			subject,
			action,
			object,
		)
		st := status.New(codes.PermissionDenied, msg)
		return st.Err()
	}
	return nil
}
```

In this code, we define an Authorizer type whose sole method, Authorize, defers to Casbin's Enforce function. This function returns whether the given subject is permitted to run the given action on the given object based on the model and policy you configure Casbin with. The New function's model and policy arguments are paths to the files where you've defined the model (which will configure Casbin's authorization mechanism—which for us will be ACL) and the policy (which is a CSV file containing your ACL table).

Because we're testing authorization, we need multiple clients with different permissions and hence multiple client certs. Having multiple clients with different permissions lets us check whether the server permits or denies a client's request based on the rules defined in the ACL. So let's change the cert generation code in your Makefile to generate multiple client certs. To do that, in the gencert target of your Makefile, replace the client cert section to look like this:

SecureYourServices/Makefile
```
cfssl gencert \
	-ca=ca.pem \
	-ca-key=ca-key.pem \
	-config=test/ca-config.json \
	-profile=client \
	-cn="root" \
	test/client-csr.json | cfssljson -bare root-client

cfssl gencert \
	-ca=ca.pem \
	-ca-key=ca-key.pem \
	-config=test/ca-config.json \
	-profile=client \
	-cn="nobody" \
	test/client-csr.json | cfssljson -bare nobody-client
```

Then run $ make gencert to generate the certs.

Now let's update our server tests to test for authorization and check that the tests fail (since our server doesn't have authorization support yet). Later, when we implement authorization in our server, the tests will pass, and we'll know we've successfully implemented authorization in the server.

First, let's update our client setup in our tests to build two clients we can use for testing our authorization setup. Update your client setup code in server_test.go to look like this:

SecureYourServices/internal/server/server_test.go

```
newClient := func(crtPath, keyPath string) (
	*grpc.ClientConn,
	api.LogClient,
	[]grpc.DialOption,
) {
	tlsConfig, err := config.SetupTLSConfig(config.TLSConfig{
		CertFile: crtPath,
		KeyFile:  keyPath,
		CAFile:   config.CAFile,
		Server:   false,
	})
	require.NoError(t, err)
	tlsCreds := credentials.NewTLS(tlsConfig)
	opts := []grpc.DialOption{grpc.WithTransportCredentials(tlsCreds)}
	conn, err := grpc.Dial(l.Addr().String(), opts...)
	require.NoError(t, err)
	client := api.NewLogClient(conn)
	return conn, client, opts
}

var rootConn *grpc.ClientConn
rootConn, rootClient, _ = newClient(
	config.RootClientCertFile,
	config.RootClientKeyFile,
)

var nobodyConn *grpc.ClientConn
nobodyConn, nobodyClient, _ = newClient(
	config.NobodyClientCertFile,
	config.NobodyClientKeyFile,
)
```

And update the teardown function to close the client connections:

SecureYourServices/internal/server/server_test.go

```
return rootClient, nobodyClient, cfg, func() {
	server.Stop()
	rootConn.Close()
	nobodyConn.Close()
	l.Close()
}
```

We're creating two clients: a superuser[9] client called root who's permitted to produce and consume, and a nobody[10] client who isn't permitted to do anything. Because the code for creating both clients is the same (aside from which cert and key they're configured with), we've refactored the client creation code into a newClient(crtPath, keyPath string) helper function. Our server now takes in an Authorizer instance that the server will defer its authorization logic to. And we pass both our root and nobody clients to the test functions so they can use whatever client they need based on whether they're testing how the server works with an authorized or unauthorized client. This last change also requires us to make some changes to our existing tests, so let's fix those.

Change your TestServer() function to the following so your test functions take in the unauthorized client:

SecureYourServices/internal/server/server_test.go

```
func TestServer(t *testing.T) {
	for scenario, fn := range map[string]func(
		t *testing.T,
		rootClient api.LogClient,
		nobodyClient api.LogClient,
		config *Config,
	){
		// ...
	} {
		t.Run(scenario, func(t *testing.T) {
			rootClient,
				nobodyClient,
				config,
				teardown := setupTest(t, nil)
			defer teardown()
			fn(t, rootClient, nobodyClient, config)
		})
	}
}
```

We need to update our existing tests to handle the second client, which we do by changing the arguments of your test functions to the following:

```
t *testing.T, client, _ api.LogClient, cfg *Config
```

We also need to add more variables to specify the locations of our nobody client's cert and key, along with the configuration files for Casbin. So add these variables to your var declaration in internal/config/files.go:

9. https://en.wikipedia.org/wiki/Superuser
10. https://en.wikipedia.org/wiki/Nobody_(username)

SecureYourServices/internal/config/files.go

```
var (
	CAFile                = configFile("ca.pem")
	ServerCertFile        = configFile("server.pem")
	ServerKeyFile         = configFile("server-key.pem")
	RootClientCertFile    = configFile("root-client.pem")
	RootClientKeyFile     = configFile("root-client-key.pem")
	NobodyClientCertFile  = configFile("nobody-client.pem")
	NobodyClientKeyFile   = configFile("nobody-client-key.pem")
	ACLModelFile          = configFile("model.conf")
	ACLPolicyFile         = configFile("policy.csv")
)
```

Since the ACL policy is specific and used throughout our tests, we'll put our Casbin configuration in the test directory as well. Inside the test directory, create a file called model.conf with the following configuration:

SecureYourServices/test/model.conf

```
# Request definition
[request_definition]
r = sub, obj, act

# Policy definition
[policy_definition]
p = sub, obj, act

# Policy effect
[policy_effect]
e = some(where (p.eft == allow))

# Matchers
[matchers]
m = r.sub == p.sub && r.obj == p.obj && r.act == p.act
```

This configures Casbin to use ACL as its authorization mechanism.

Alongside the model.conf file, add a policy.csv file with this snippet:

SecureYourServices/test/policy.csv

```
p, root, *, produce
p, root, *, consume
```

This is your ACL table, with two entries saying that the root client has produce and consume permissions on the * object (which we're using as a wildcard, meaning any object). All other clients, including nobody, will be denied.

Now we need to install the policy and model files into the CONFIG_PATH so our tests can find them. Update your Makefile's test target to the following:

SecureYourServices/Makefile

```
$(CONFIG_PATH)/model.conf:
	cp test/model.conf $(CONFIG_PATH)/model.conf

$(CONFIG_PATH)/policy.csv:
	cp test/policy.csv $(CONFIG_PATH)/policy.csv

.PHONY: test
test: $(CONFIG_PATH)/policy.csv $(CONFIG_PATH)/model.conf
	go test -race ./...
```

Now your tests are in a runnable state again, so you can run `$ make test` to see that they still pass! This is because the existing tests use the root client, which is authorized to produce and consume, and our current tests assume the client is authorized, and so they pass.

Let's add a test to check that unauthorized clients are denied. In `server_test.go`, import these packages:

SecureYourServices/internal/server/server_test.go

```
"google.golang.org/grpc/codes"
"google.golang.org/grpc/status"
```

Below the `testProduceConsumeStream()` test we added in the last chapter, add this `testUnauthorized()` test:

SecureYourServices/internal/server/server_test.go

```
func testUnauthorized(
	t *testing.T,
	_,
	client api.LogClient,
	config *Config,
) {
	ctx := context.Background()
	produce, err := client.Produce(ctx,
		&api.ProduceRequest{
			Record: &api.Record{
				Value: []byte("hello world"),
			},
		},
	)
	if produce != nil {
		t.Fatalf("produce response should be nil")
	}
	gotCode, wantCode := status.Code(err), codes.PermissionDenied
	if gotCode != wantCode {
		t.Fatalf("got code: %d, want: %d", gotCode, wantCode)
	}
	consume, err := client.Consume(ctx, &api.ConsumeRequest{
		Offset: 0,
	})
```

```
        if consume != nil {
                t.Fatalf("consume response should be nil")
        }
        gotCode, wantCode = status.Code(err), codes.PermissionDenied
        if gotCode != wantCode {
                t.Fatalf("got code: %d, want: %d", gotCode, wantCode)
        }
}
```

In this test, we use the nobody client, which isn't permitted to do anything. We try to use the client to produce and consume, just as we did in the successful test case. Since our client isn't authorized, we want our server to deny the client, which we verify by checking the code on the returned error.

Update the test table in TestServer(*testing.T) to include our unauthorized test by adding the highlighted line:

SecureYourServices/internal/server/server_test.go

```
"produce/consume a message to/from the log succeeeds": testProduceConsume,
"produce/consume stream succeeds":                     testProduceConsumeStream,
"consume past log boundary fails":                     testConsumePastBoundary,
"unauthorized fails": testUnauthorized,
```

If we run our tests with $ make test, they'll fail because our server is still permitting all clients to do anything, since we haven't hooked up its authorization yet. Let's add authorization to the server now.

Update your Config in server.go, update your imports to the following:

SecureYourServices/internal/server/server.go

```
import (
        "context"

        api "github.com/travisjeffery/proglog/api/v1"

        grpc_middleware "github.com/grpc-ecosystem/go-grpc-middleware"
        grpc_auth "github.com/grpc-ecosystem/go-grpc-middleware/auth"
        "google.golang.org/grpc"
        "google.golang.org/grpc/credentials"
        "google.golang.org/grpc/codes"
        "google.golang.org/grpc/peer"
        "google.golang.org/grpc/status"
)
```

Now we'll add a field for the authorizer and some constants we will use for authorization:

SecureYourServices/internal/server/server.go

```
type Config struct {
        CommitLog  CommitLog
        Authorizer Authorizer
}
```

```
const (
        objectWildcard = "*"
        produceAction  = "produce"
        consumeAction  = "consume"
)
```

The constants match the values we in our ACL policy table, and we'll reference them a few times in this file so they make sense being constants. The Config's Authorizer field is an interface we need to define; put the following snippet below the CommitLog interface:

SecureYourServices/internal/server/server.go

```
type Authorizer interface {
        Authorize(subject, object, action string) error
}
```

We depend on an interface for the Authorizer so that we can switch out the authorization implementation—same as the CommitLog in Dependency Inversion with Interfaces, on page 67. Update your Produce() method to this snippet, adding the highlighted lines:

SecureYourServices/internal/server/server.go

```
func (s *grpcServer) Produce(ctx context.Context, req *api.ProduceRequest) (
        *api.ProduceResponse, error) {
➤       if err := s.Authorizer.Authorize(
➤               subject(ctx),
➤               objectWildcard,
➤               produceAction,
➤       ); err != nil {
➤               return nil, err
➤       }
        offset, err := s.CommitLog.Append(req.Record)
        if err != nil {
                return nil, err
        }
        return &api.ProduceResponse{Offset: offset}, nil
}
```

Make a similar change to your Consume() method, changing the method to this:

SecureYourServices/internal/server/server.go

```
func (s *grpcServer) Consume(ctx context.Context, req *api.ConsumeRequest) (
        *api.ConsumeResponse, error) {
➤       if err := s.Authorizer.Authorize(
➤               subject(ctx),
➤               objectWildcard,
➤               consumeAction,
➤       ); err != nil {
➤               return nil, err
➤       }
```

```
        record, err := s.CommitLog.Read(req.Offset)
        if err != nil {
                return nil, err
        }
        return &api.ConsumeResponse{Record: record}, nil
}
```

We now have the server checking whether the client (identified by the cert's subject) is authorized to produce and consume, and if not, sending the permission denied error back to the client. When producing, if the client is authorized, then the method will continue and append the given record to the log. And when consuming, if the client is authorized, then the method will consume the record from the log. We take the subject out of the client's cert with two helper functions. Add the following code at the bottom of server.go:

SecureYourServices/internal/server/server.go

```
func authenticate(ctx context.Context) (context.Context, error) {
        peer, ok := peer.FromContext(ctx)
        if !ok {
                return ctx, status.New(
                        codes.Unknown,
                        "couldn't find peer info",
                ).Err()
        }

        if peer.AuthInfo == nil {
                return context.WithValue(ctx, subjectContextKey{}, ""), nil
        }

        tlsInfo := peer.AuthInfo.(credentials.TLSInfo)
        subject := tlsInfo.State.VerifiedChains[0][0].Subject.CommonName
        ctx = context.WithValue(ctx, subjectContextKey{}, subject)

        return ctx, nil
}

func subject(ctx context.Context) string {
        return ctx.Value(subjectContextKey{}).(string)
}

type subjectContextKey struct{}
```

The authenticate(context.Context) function is an interceptor that reads the subject out of the client's cert and writes it to the RPC's context. With interceptors, you can intercept and modify the execution of each RPC call, allowing you to break the request handling into smaller, reusable chunks. (Other frameworks name the same concept *middleware*.) The subject(context.Context) function returns the client's cert's subject so we can identify a client and check their access.

Update your NewGRPCServer(*Config, ...grpc.ServerOption) function to the following code:

SecureYourServices/internal/server/server.go
```
func NewGRPCServer(config *Config, opts ...grpc.ServerOption) (
	*grpc.Server,
	error,
) {
	opts = append(opts, grpc.StreamInterceptor(
		grpc_middleware.ChainStreamServer(
			grpc_auth.StreamServerInterceptor(authenticate),
		)), grpc.UnaryInterceptor(grpc_middleware.ChainUnaryServer(
		grpc_auth.UnaryServerInterceptor(authenticate),
	)))
	gsrv := grpc.NewServer(opts...)
	srv, err := newgrpcServer(config)
	if err != nil {
		return nil, err
	}
	api.RegisterLogServer(gsrv, srv)
	return gsrv, nil
}
```

We hook up our authenticate() interceptor to our gRPC server so that our server identifies the subject of each RPC to kick off the authorization process.

Now update your test server's configuration to pass in an authorizer. In setup_test.go's setupTest, import your auth package, and update the server's configuration to the following:

SecureYourServices/internal/server/server_test.go
```
authorizer := auth.New(config.ACLModelFile, config.ACLPolicyFile)
cfg = &Config{
	CommitLog:  clog,
	Authorizer: authorizer,
}
```

Our server now authorizes its requests! You can verify that everything works by running the tests again: $ make test. Last time we ran them they failed because our server didn't deny the nobody client who doesn't have any permissions. This time the tests pass since our server will now only authorize users who are permitted based on your ACL!

What You Learned

You've learned how to secure services in three parts: by encrypting connections with TLS, through mutual TLS authentication to verify the identities of clients and servers, and by using ACL-based authorization to permit client actions. Next we'll make our service observable by adding metrics, logs, and traces.

CHAPTER 6

Observe Your Systems

Imagine waking up one day and noticing that the last hole in your belt doesn't fit. You head to your scale and you see that you've gained a significant amount of weight overnight. You go on an emergency diet and fitness regimen. A couple of weeks later, you check the scales and see you gained even more weight somehow. What's going on?

What you need is insight into what's going on in your body. If our body had built-in observability, we'd have metrics on our body, like hormone levels that we could graph on a dashboard. If we could see a sudden imbalance in our hormone levels, with all things being equal, we could surmise that a hormonal imbalance must be the root cause. But without being able to see what had changed, you'd make many changes in search of the problem, each with their own effects.

We make our systems observable so we can we can ask questions that will give us insight into the system and debug unexpected problems. The keyword is *unexpected*—making our system observable means we can fix arbitrary problems that haven't happened before. In this chapter, we'll make our service observable so we understand what's going on within it.

Three Types of Telemetry Data

Observability is a measure of how well we understand our system's internals—its behavior and state—from its external outputs. We use metrics, structured logs, and traces as the outputs to make our systems observable. While there are three types of telemetry data, each with its own use case we'll talk about, it'll often derive from the same events. For example, each time a web service handles a request, it may increment a "requests handled" metric, emit a log for the request, and make a trace.

Metrics

Metrics measure numeric data over time, such as how many requests failed or how long each request took. Metrics like these help to define service-level indicators (SLI), objectives (SLO), and agreements (SLA). You'll use metrics to report the health of your system, trigger internal alerts, and graph on dashboards to get an idea of how your system's doing at a glance.

Because metrics are numerical data, you can gradually reduce resolution to reduce the storage requirements and time to query. For example, if we ran a book publishing company, we'd have metrics on each book purchase. To ship a customer's books, we'd need to know the customer's order, but after we've delivered the books and the return policy has passed, we don't care about the order anymore. When we're doing accounting or analysis on our business, that's too much detail. Eventually we'd only need quarterly earnings to do our taxes, calculate year-over-year growth, and know if we can hire more editors and authors to expand our business.

There are three kinds of metrics:

Counters

Counters track the number of times an event happened, such as the number of requests that failed or the sum of some fact of your system like the number of bytes processed.

You'll often take a counter and use it to get a rate: the number of times an event happened in an interval. Who cares about the total requests we've received other than to brag about it? What we care about is how many requests we've handled in the past second or minute—if that dropped significantly you'd want to check for latency in your system. You'd want to know when your request error rate spikes so you can see what's wrong and fix it.

Histograms

Histograms show you a distribution of your data. You'll mainly use histograms for measuring the percentiles of your request duration and sizes.

Gauges

Gauges track the current value of something. You can replace that value entirely. Gauges are useful for saturation-type metrics, like a host's disk usage percentage or the number of load balancers compared to your cloud provider's limits.

You could measure just about anything, so what data should you measure? What metrics will provide worthy signals on your system? These are Google's four golden signals[1] to measure:

- *Latency*—the time it takes your service to process requests. If your latency spikes, you often need to scale your system vertically by changing to an instance with more memory, CPUs, or IOPS, or scale your system horizontally by adding more instances to your load balancer.
- *Traffic*—the amount of demand on your service. For a typical web service, this could be requests processed per second. For an online video game or video streaming service, it could be the number of concurrent users. These metrics are good for bragging rights (hopefully), but more important, they can help give you an idea of the scale at which you're working and when you've scaled to the point you need a new design.
- *Errors*—your service's request failure rate. Internal server errors are particularly important.
- *Saturation*—a measure of your service's capacity. For example, if your service persists data to disk, at your current ingress rate will you run out of hard drive space soon? If you have an in-memory store, how much memory is your service using compared to the memory available?

While most debugging stories begin with metrics—either through an alert or someone noticing abnormalities on the dashboard—you'll go to your logs and traces to learn more details about the problem. Let's take a look at those next.

Structured Logs

Logs describe events in your system. You should log any event that gives you useful insight into your service. Logs should help us troubleshoot, audit, and profile so we can learn what went wrong and why, who ran what actions, and how long those actions took. For example, a gRPC service log could log this per RPC call:

```
{
  "request_id": "f47ac10b-58cc-0372-8567-0e02b2c3d479",
  "level": "info",
  "ts": 1600139560.3399575,
  "caller": "zap/server_interceptors.go:67",
  "msg": "finished streaming call with code OK",
  "peer.address": "127.0.0.1:54304",
```

1. https://landing.google.com/sre/sre-book/chapters/monitoring-distributed-systems/#xref_monitoring_golden-signals

```
  "grpc.start_time": "2020-09-14T22:12:40-05:00",
  "system": "grpc",
  "span.kind": "server",
  "grpc.service": "log.v1.Log",
  "grpc.method": "ConsumeStream",
  "peer.address": "127.0.0.1:54304",
  "grpc.code": "OK",
  "grpc.time_ns": 197740
}
```


In this log we see when the caller called the method, the caller's IP address, the service and method they called, if the call succeeded, and how long the request took. In distributed systems, the request ID is helpful for piecing together a complete picture of a request that's handled by multiple services.

This gRPC log is a JSON formatted, structured log. A structured log is a set of name and value ordered pairs encoded in consistent schema and format that's easily read by programs. Structured logs enable us to separate log capturing, transporting, persisting, and querying. For example, we could capture and transport our logs as protocol buffers and then re-encode them in the Parquet[2] format and persist them in your columnar database.

I recommend collecting your structured logs in an event streaming platform like Kafka to enable arbitrary processing and transporting of your logs. For example, you can connect Kafka with a database like BigQuery to query your logs while connecting Kafka with an object store like GCS to maintain historical copies.

At play is a balance between logging too little and being without the information needed to debug a problem, or logging too much and being overwhelmed by too much information and missing what's important. I suggest erring on logging too much, and cut back on the logs that aren't useful as you learn more. That way you're less likely to be without information you need to troubleshoot or audit a problem.

Traces

Traces capture request lifecycles and let you track requests as they flow through your system. Tracing user interfaces like Jaegar,[3] Stackdriver,[4] and Lightstep[5] give you a visual representation of where requests spend time in your system. In distributed systems, this is especially useful as requests

2. https://parquet.apache.org
3. https://www.jaegertracing.io
4. https://cloud.google.com/products/operations
5. https://lightstep.com

execute over multiple services. The following screenshot shows an example of a trace of Jocko's request handling in Jaegar.

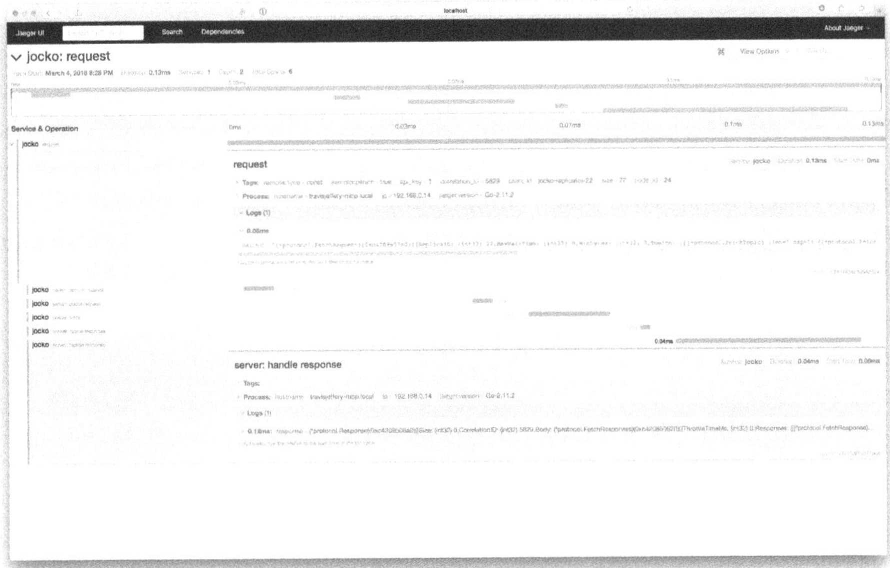

You can tag your traces with details to know more about each request. A common example is tagging each trace with a user ID so that if users experience a problem, you can easily find their requests.

Traces comprise one or more *spans*. Spans can have parent/child relationships or be linked as siblings. Each span represents a part of the request's execution. How detailed you break up those parts is up to you. Go wide to begin: trace requests across all your services end-to-end, with spans that begin and end at the entry and exit points of your services. Then go deep in each service and trace important method calls.

Now, let's update our code to make your service observable.

Make Your Service Observable

Let's make your service observable by adding metrics, structured logs, and traces. When you deploy your services to production, you'll usually configure your metrics, structured logs, and traces to go to external services like Prometheus,[6] Elasticsearch,[7] and Jaegar. To keep things simple, we'll just log our observability pieces to files and see what the data looks like.

6. https://prometheus.io
7. https://www.elastic.co/elasticsearch

OpenTelemetry[8] is a Cloud Native Computing Foundation (CNCF) project that provides robust and portable APIs and libraries that we can use for metrics and distributed tracing in our service. (OpenCensus and OpenTracing merged to form OpenTelemetry, which is backward-compatible with existing OpenCensus integrations.) OpenTelemetry's Go gRPC integration supports traces but not metrics, so we'll use the OpenCensus libraries in our service since OpenCensus's gRPC integration supports them both. Unfortunately, neither OpenTelemetry nor OpenCensus support logging yet. OpenTelemetry should support logging at some point—a special interest group[9] is planning OpenTelemetry's logging specification. In the meantime, we'll use Uber's Zap logging library.[10]

Most Go networking APIs support middleware, so you can wrap request handling with your own logic. This is where I recommend beginning making your service observable by wrapping all requests with metrics, logs, and traces. That's why we're using the OpenCensus and Zap integrations' interceptors.

Run the following commands within your project to add the OpenCensus and Zap dependencies:

```
$ go get go.uber.org/zap@v1.10.0
$ go get go.opencensus.io@v0.22.2
```

Then open internal/server/server.go and update your imports to include the highlighted imports in this snippet:

ObserveYourServices/internal/server/server.go

```
import (
	"context"

	grpc_middleware "github.com/grpc-ecosystem/go-grpc-middleware"
	grpc_auth "github.com/grpc-ecosystem/go-grpc-middleware/auth"
	api "github.com/travisjeffery/proglog/api/v1"

➤	"time"
➤
➤	grpc_zap "github.com/grpc-ecosystem/go-grpc-middleware/logging/zap"
➤	grpc_ctxtags "github.com/grpc-ecosystem/go-grpc-middleware/tags"
➤	"go.opencensus.io/plugin/ocgrpc"
➤	"go.opencensus.io/stats/view"
➤	"go.opencensus.io/trace"
➤	"go.uber.org/zap"
➤	"go.uber.org/zap/zapcore"
```

8. https://opentelemetry.io
9. https://github.com/open-telemetry/community#logs-working-group
10. https://github.com/uber-go/zap

```
        "google.golang.org/grpc"
        "google.golang.org/grpc/codes"
        "google.golang.org/grpc/credentials"
        "google.golang.org/grpc/peer"
        "google.golang.org/grpc/status"
)
```

Now update NewGRPCServer() to configure Zap:

ObserveYourServices/internal/server/server.go

```
func NewGRPCServer(config *Config, grpcOpts ...grpc.ServerOption) (
        *grpc.Server,
        error,
) {
        logger := zap.L().Named("server")
        zapOpts := []grpc_zap.Option{
                grpc_zap.WithDurationField(
                        func(duration time.Duration) zapcore.Field {
                                return zap.Int64(
                                        "grpc.time_ns",
                                        duration.Nanoseconds(),
                                )
                        },
                ),
        }
```

We specify the logger's name to differentiate the server logs from other logs in our service. Then we add a "grpc.time_ns" field to our structured logs to log the duration of each request in nanoseconds.

After the previous snippet, add the following snippet to configure how OpenCensus collects metrics and traces:

ObserveYourServices/internal/server/server.go

```
trace.ApplyConfig(trace.Config{DefaultSampler: trace.AlwaysSample()})
err := view.Register(ocgrpc.DefaultServerViews...)
if err != nil {
        return nil, err
}
```

We've configured OpenCensus to always sample the traces because we're developing our service and we want all of our requests traced.

In production you may not want to trace every request because it could affect performance, require too much data, or trace confidential data. If tracing too much is the problem, you can use the probability sampler and sample a percentage of the requests. However, one problem with using the probability sampler is that you may miss important requests. We could try to reconcile these trade-offs by writing our own sampler that always traces important requests and samples a percentage of the rest of the requests. The code for that would look like this:

```
halfSampler := trace.ProbabilitySampler(0.5)
trace.ApplyConfig(trace.Config{
	DefaultSampler: func(p trace.SamplingParameters) trace.SamplingDecision {
		if strings.Contains(p.Name, "Produce"){
			return trace.SamplingDecision{Sample: true}
		}
		return halfSampler(p)
	},
})
```

The views specify what stats OpenCensus will collect. The default server views track stats on:

- Received bytes per RPC
- Sent bytes per RPC
- Latency
- Completed RPCs

Now, change the grpcOpts after the previous snippet to include the lines highlighted here:

ObserveYourServices/internal/server/server.go

```
grpcOpts = append(grpcOpts,
	grpc.StreamInterceptor(
		grpc_middleware.ChainStreamServer(
			grpc_ctxtags.StreamServerInterceptor(),
			grpc_zap.StreamServerInterceptor(logger, zapOpts...),
			grpc_auth.StreamServerInterceptor(authenticate),
		)), grpc.UnaryInterceptor(grpc_middleware.ChainUnaryServer(
		grpc_ctxtags.UnaryServerInterceptor(),
		grpc_zap.UnaryServerInterceptor(logger, zapOpts...),
		grpc_auth.UnaryServerInterceptor(authenticate),
	)),
	grpc.StatsHandler(&ocgrpc.ServerHandler{}),
)
```

These lines configure gRPC to apply the Zap interceptors that log the gRPC calls and attach OpenCensus as the server's stat handler so that OpenCensus can record stats on the server's request handling.

Okay, now we just have to change our test setup to configure the metrics and traces log files. Open internal/server/server_test.go and add these imports:

ObserveYourServices/internal/server/server_test.go

```
"os"
"time"
"flag"
```

```
"go.opencensus.io/examples/exporter"
"go.uber.org/zap"
```

Below your imports, add this snippet that defines a debug flag to enable observability output:

ObserveYourServices/internal/server/server_test.go

```
// imports...
var debug = flag.Bool("debug", false, "Enable observability for debugging.")

func TestMain(m *testing.M) {
	flag.Parse()
	if *debug {
		logger, err := zap.NewDevelopment()
		if err != nil {
			panic(err)
		}
		zap.ReplaceGlobals(logger)
	}
	os.Exit(m.Run())
}
```

When a test file implements TestMain(m *testing.M), Go will call TestMain(m) instead of running the tests directly. TestMain() gives us a place for setup that applies to all tests in that file, like enabling our debug output. Flag parsing has to go in TestMain() instead of init(), otherwise Go can't define the flag and your code will error and exit.

In the setupTest() function, after the authorizer variable, add this snippet:

ObserveYourServices/internal/server/server_test.go

```
var telemetryExporter *exporter.LogExporter
if *debug {
	metricsLogFile, err := ioutil.TempFile("", "metrics-*.log")
	require.NoError(t, err)
	t.Logf("metrics log file: %s", metricsLogFile.Name())

	tracesLogFile, err := ioutil.TempFile("", "traces-*.log")
	require.NoError(t, err)
	t.Logf("traces log file: %s", tracesLogFile.Name())

	telemetryExporter, err = exporter.NewLogExporter(exporter.Options{
		MetricsLogFile:    metricsLogFile.Name(),
		TracesLogFile:     tracesLogFile.Name(),
		ReportingInterval: time.Second,
	})
	require.NoError(t, err)
	err = telemetryExporter.Start()
	require.NoError(t, err)
}
```

This snippet sets up and starts the telemetry exporter to write to two files. Each test gets its own separate trace and metrics files so we can see each test's requests.

At the bottom of setupTest(), update the teardown function to include these highlighted lines:

ObserveYourServices/internal/server/server_test.go
```
return rootClient, nobodyClient, cfg, func() {
	server.Stop()
	rootConn.Close()
	nobodyConn.Close()
	l.Close()
	if telemetryExporter != nil {
		time.Sleep(1500 * time.Millisecond)
		telemetryExporter.Stop()
		telemetryExporter.Close()
	}
}
```

We sleep for 1.5 seconds to give the telemetry exporter enough time to flush its data to disk. Then we stop and close the exporter.

Run your server tests by navigating into the internal/server directory and executing this command:

```
$ go test -v -debug=true
```

In the test output, find these metrics and traces file logs, and open them to see the exported metrics and trace data:

```
metrics log file: /tmp/metrics-{{random string}}.log
traces log file: /tmp/traces-{{random string}}.log
```

For example, here's the completed RPC stat showing that the server handled two successful produce calls:

```
Metric: name: grpc.io/server/completed_rpcs, type: TypeCumulativeInt64, unit: ms
  Labels: [
    {grpc_server_method}={log.v1.Log/Produce true}
    {grpc_server_status}={OK true}]
    Value : value=2
```

And here's a trace for a produce call:

```
TraceID:      3e3343b74193e6a807cac515e82fb3b3
SpanID:       045493d1be3f7188

Span:    log.v1.Log.Produce
Status:   [0]
Elapsed: 1ms
SpanKind: Server
```

```
Attributes:
  - Client=false
  - FailFast=false

MessageEvents:
Received
UncompressedByteSize: 15
CompressedByteSize: 0

Sent
UncompressedByteSize: 0
CompressedByteSize: 5
```

We can now observe what's going on in our service!

What You Learned

In this chapter, you learned about observability and its role in making reliable systems. You'll find tracing especially useful in distributed systems, as it gives you a complete story of requests that take part over multiple services. You also learned how to make your service observable. Next, we'll make our server support clustering to the service highly available and scalable.

Part III

Distribute

CHAPTER 7

Server-to-Server Service Discovery

So far we've built a secure, stand-alone gRPC web service. Now let's start our journey toward making our stand-alone service into a distributed one by incorporating service discovery so that our service automatically handles when a node is added to or removed from our cluster.

If you're not familiar with service discovery, don't worry—you will be after reading this chapter. Service discovery is one of the coolest things about distributed services: machines automatically discovering other machines! (When Skynet becomes self aware and takes over, we can thank service discovery for playing a part.) Here's a quick overview of the many benefits of service discovery.

Why Use Service Discovery?

Service discovery is the process of figuring out how to connect to a service. A service discovery solution must keep an up-to-date list (also known as a *registry*) of services, their locations, and their health. Downstream services then query this registry to discover the location of upstream services and connect to them—for example, a web service discovering and connecting to its database. This way, even if the upstream services change (scale up or down, or get replaced), downstream services can still connect to them.

In the pre-cloud days, you could set up "service discovery" with manually managed and configured static addresses, which was workable since applications ran on static hardware. Today, service discovery plays a big part in modern cloud applications where nodes change frequently.

Instead of using service discovery, some developers put load balancers in front of their services so that the load balancers provide static IPs. But for server-to-server communication, where you control the servers and you don't need a load balancer to act as a trust boundary[1] between clients and servers, use service discovery instead. Load balancers add cost, increase latency, introduce single points of failure, and need updates as services scale up and down. If you manage tens or hundreds of microservices, then not using service discovery means you also have to manage tens or hundreds of load balancers and DNS records. For a distributed service like ours, using a load balancer would force us to depend on a load-balancer service like nginx or the various cloud load balancers like AWS's ELB or Google Cloud's Load Balancer. This would increase our operational burden, infrastructure costs, and latency.

In our system, we have two service-discovery problems to solve:

- How will the servers in our cluster discover each other?
- How will the clients discover the servers?

In this chapter, we'll work on implementing the discovery for the servers. Then, after we implement consensus in Chapter 8, Coordinate Your Services with Consensus, on page 141, we'll work on the clients' discovery in Chapter 9, Discover Servers and Load Balance from the Client, on page 171.

Now that you know what service discovery can do, we're ready to embed it into our service.

Embed Service Discovery

When you have an application that needs to talk to a service, the tool you use for service discovery needs to perform the following tasks:

- Manage a registry of services containing info such as their IPs and ports;
- Help services find other services using the registry;
- Health check service instances and remove them if they're not well; and
- Deregister services when they go offline.

Historically, people who've built distributed services have depended on separate, stand-alone services for service discovery (such as Consul, ZooKeeper, and Etcd). In this architecture, users of your service run two clusters: one for your service and one for your service discovery. The benefit of using a service-discovery service is that you don't have to build service discovery yourself. The downside to using such a service, from your users' standpoint, is that they have to learn, launch, and operate an extra service's cluster. So using a stand-alone service for discovery removes the burden from your shoulders and puts it on your users'. That means many users won't use your

1. https://en.wikipedia.org/wiki/Trust_boundary

service because the burden is too much for them, and users who *do* take it on won't recommend your service to others as often or as highly.

So why did people who built distributed services use stand-alone service-discovery services, and why did their users put up with the extra burden? Because neither had much of a choice. The people building distributed services didn't have the libraries they needed to embed service discovery into their services, and users didn't have other options.

Fortunately, times have changed. Today, Gophers have Serf—a library that provides decentralized cluster membership, failure detection, and orchestration that you can use to easily embed service discovery into your distributed services. Hashicorp, the company that created it, uses Serf to power its own service-discovery product, Consul, so you're in good company.

Using Serf to embed service discovery into your services means that you don't have to implement service discovery yourself and your users don't have to run an extra cluster. It's a win-win.

When to Depend on a Stand-Alone Service-Discovery Solution

You may encounter cases where depending on a stand-alone service for service discovery makes sense—for example, if you need to integrate your service discovery with many platforms. You sink a lot of effort into that kind of work, and that's likely a poor use of your time when you could just use a service like Consul that provides those integrations. In any case, Serf is always a good place to start. Once you've developed your service to solve the core problem it's targeting and your service is stable or close to it, then you will have a good sense of whether you need to depend on a service-discovery service.

Here are some other benefits of building our service with Serf:

- In the early days of building a service, Serf is faster to set up and build our service against than having to set up a separate service.
- It's easier to move from Serf to a stand-alone service than to move from a stand-alone service to Serf, so we still have both options open.
- Our service will be easier and more flexible to deploy, making our service more accessible.

So for our service, we'll use Serf to build service discovery.

Now that we've seen the benefits of using Serf, let's quickly discuss how Serf does its thing.

Discover Services with Serf

Serf maintains cluster membership by using an efficient, lightweight gossip protocol to communicate between the service's nodes. Unlike service registry projects like ZooKeeper and Consul, Serf doesn't have a central-registry architectural style. Instead, each instance of your service in the cluster runs as a Serf node. These nodes exchange messages with each other in the same way a zombie apocalypse might occur: one infected zombie soon spreads to infect everyone else. With Serf, instead of a spreading zombie virus, you're spreading information about the nodes in your cluster. You listen to Serf for messages about changes in the cluster and then handle them accordingly.

To implement service discovery with Serf we need to:

1. Create a Serf node on each server.
2. Configure each Serf node with an address to listen on and accept connections from other Serf nodes.
3. Configure each Serf node with addresses of other Serf nodes and join their cluster.
4. Handle Serf's cluster discovery events, such as when a node joins or fails in the cluster.

Let's get coding.

Serf is a lightweight tool that you can use for infinite use cases, but its API can be verbose when you have a specific problem to solve. The specific job we want our discovery layer to solve is to tell us when a server joined or left the cluster and what its ID and address are with as little API as possible. So let's make a discovery package our server will use.

To get started, install the Serf package by running this command:

```
$ go get github.com/hashicorp/serf@v0.8.5
```

Then create an internal/discovery directory and inside it create a membership.go file, beginning with this code:

ServerSideServiceDiscovery/internal/discovery/membership.go

```go
package discovery

import (
	"net"

	"go.uber.org/zap"

	"github.com/hashicorp/serf/serf"
)
```

```
type Membership struct {
	Config
	handler Handler
	serf    *serf.Serf
	events  chan serf.Event
	logger  *zap.Logger
}

func New(handler Handler, config Config) (*Membership, error) {
	c := &Membership{
		Config:  config,
		handler: handler,
		logger:  zap.L().Named("membership"),
	}
	if err := c.setupSerf(); err != nil {
		return nil, err
	}
	return c, nil
}
```

Membership is our type wrapping Serf to provide discovery and cluster membership to our service. Users will call New() to create a Membership with the required configuration and event handler.

Add this code below the New() function to define the configuration type and set up Serf:

ServerSideServiceDiscovery/internal/discovery/membership.go

```
type Config struct {
	NodeName       string
	BindAddr       string
	Tags           map[string]string
	StartJoinAddrs []string
}

func (m *Membership) setupSerf() (err error) {
	addr, err := net.ResolveTCPAddr("tcp", m.BindAddr)
	if err != nil {
		return err
	}
	config := serf.DefaultConfig()
	config.Init()
	config.MemberlistConfig.BindAddr = addr.IP.String()
	config.MemberlistConfig.BindPort = addr.Port
	m.events = make(chan serf.Event)
	config.EventCh = m.events
	config.Tags = m.Tags
	config.NodeName = m.Config.NodeName
	m.serf, err = serf.Create(config)
	if err != nil {
		return err
	}
```

```
        go m.eventHandler()
        if m.StartJoinAddrs != nil {
                _, err = m.serf.Join(m.StartJoinAddrs, true)
                if err != nil {
                        return err
                }
        }
        return nil
}
```

Serf has a lot of configurable parameters, but the five parameters you'll typically use are:

- NodeName—the node name acts as the node's unique identifier across the Serf cluster. If you don't set the node name, Serf uses the hostname.
- BindAddr and BindPort—Serf listens on this address and port for gossiping.
- Tags—Serf shares these tags to the other nodes in the cluster and should use these tags for simple data that informs the cluster how to handle this node. For example, Consul shares each node's RPC address with Serf tags, and once they know each other's RPC address, they can make RPCs to each other. Consul shares whether the node is a voter or non-voter, which changes the node's role in the Raft cluster. We'll talk about this more in the next chapter when we use Raft to build consensus in our cluster. In our code, similar to Consul, we'll share each node's user-configured RPC address with a Serf tag so the nodes know which addresses to send their RPCs.
- EventCh—the event channel is how you'll receive Serf's events when a node joins or leaves the cluster. If you want a snapshot of the members at any point in time, you can call Serf's Members() method.
- StartJoinAddrs—when you have an existing cluster and you create a new node that you want to add to that cluster, you need to point your new node to at least one of the nodes now in the cluster. After the new node connects to one of those nodes in the existing cluster, it'll learn about the rest of the nodes, and vice versa (the existing nodes learn about the new node). The StartJoinAddrs field is how you configure new nodes to join an existing cluster. You set the field to the addresses of nodes in the cluster, and Serf's gossip protocol takes care of the rest to join your node to the cluster. In a production environment, specify at least three addresses to make your cluster resilient to one or two node failures or a disrupted network.

setupSerf() creates and configures a Serf instance and starts the eventsHandler() goroutine to handle Serf's events.

Define the Handler interface by putting this snippet below setupSerf():

ServerSideServiceDiscovery/internal/discovery/membership.go

```
type Handler interface {
	Join(name, addr string) error
	Leave(name string) error
}
```

The Handler represents some component in our service that needs to know when a server joins or leaves the cluster.

In this chapter we will build a component that replicates the data of servers that join the cluster. In the next chapter, where we will build consensus in our service, Raft needs to know when servers join the cluster to coordinate with them.

Add this snippet below Handler() to define the eventHandler() method:

ServerSideServiceDiscovery/internal/discovery/membership.go

```
func (m *Membership) eventHandler() {
	for e := range m.events {
		switch e.EventType() {
		case serf.EventMemberJoin:
			for _, member := range e.(serf.MemberEvent).Members {
				if m.isLocal(member) {
					continue
				}
				m.handleJoin(member)
			}
		case serf.EventMemberLeave, serf.EventMemberFailed:
			for _, member := range e.(serf.MemberEvent).Members {
				if m.isLocal(member) {
					return
				}
				m.handleLeave(member)
			}
		}
	}
}

func (m *Membership) handleJoin(member serf.Member) {
	if err := m.handler.Join(
		member.Name,
		member.Tags["rpc_addr"],
	); err != nil {
		m.logError(err, "failed to join", member)
	}
}

func (m *Membership) handleLeave(member serf.Member) {
	if err := m.handler.Leave(
		member.Name,
```

```
		); err != nil {
			m.logError(err, "failed to leave", member)
		}
}
```

The eventHandler() runs in a loop reading events sent by Serf into the events channel, handling each incoming event according to the event's type. When a node joins or leaves the cluster, Serf sends an event to all nodes, including the node that joined or left the cluster. We check whether the node we got an event for is the local server so the server doesn't act on itself—we don't want the server to try and replicate itself, for example.

Notice that Serf may coalesce multiple members updates into one event. For example, say ten nodes join around the same time; in that case, Serf will send you one join event with ten members, so that's why we iterate over the event's members.

Put this code below eventHandler() to implement the rest of Membership:

ServerSideServiceDiscovery/internal/discovery/membership.go

```
func (m *Membership) isLocal(member serf.Member) bool {
	return m.serf.LocalMember().Name == member.Name
}

func (m *Membership) Members() []serf.Member {
	return m.serf.Members()
}

func (m *Membership) Leave() error {
	return m.serf.Leave()
}

func (m *Membership) logError(err error, msg string, member serf.Member) {
	m.logger.Error(
		msg,
		zap.Error(err),
		zap.String("name", member.Name),
		zap.String("rpc_addr", member.Tags["rpc_addr"]),
	)
}
```

These methods comprise the rest of Membership:

- isLocal() returns whether the given Serf member is the local member by checking the members' names.
- Members() returns a point-in-time snapshot of the cluster's Serf members.
- Leave() tells this member to leave the Serf cluster.
- logError() logs the given error and message.

Let's test our Membership code now. Create a membership_test.go file in the internal/discovery directory, and begin the file with this code:

ServerSideServiceDiscovery/internal/discovery/membership_test.go

```
package discovery_test

import (
	"fmt"
	"testing"
	"time"

	"github.com/hashicorp/serf/serf"
	"github.com/stretchr/testify/require"
	"github.com/travisjeffery/go-dynaport"
	. "github.com/travisjeffery/proglog/internal/discovery"
)

func TestMembership(t *testing.T) {
	m, handler := setupMember(t, nil)
	m, _ = setupMember(t, m)
	m, _ = setupMember(t, m)

	require.Eventually(t, func() bool {
		return 2 == len(handler.joins) &&
			3 == len(m[0].Members()) &&
			0 == len(handler.leaves)
	}, 3*time.Second, 250*time.Millisecond)

	require.NoError(t, m[2].Leave())

	require.Eventually(t, func() bool {
		return 2 == len(handler.joins) &&
			3 == len(m[0].Members()) &&
			serf.StatusLeft == m[0].Members()[2].Status &&
			1 == len(handler.leaves)
	}, 3*time.Second, 250*time.Millisecond)

	require.Equal(t, fmt.Sprintf("%d", 2), <-handler.leaves)
}
```

Our test sets up a cluster with multiple servers and checks that the Membership returns all the servers that joined the membership and updates after a server leaves the cluster. The handler's joins and leaves channels tell us how many times each event happened and for what servers. Each member has a status to know how its doing:

- *Alive*—the server is present and healthy.
- *Leaving*—the server is gracefully leaving the cluster.
- *Left*—the server has gracefully left the cluster.
- *Failed*—the server unexpectedly left the cluster.

TestMembership() relies on a helper method to set up a member each time you call it. Define the helper setupMember() by adding the following code below TestMembership():

ServerSideServiceDiscovery/internal/discovery/membership_test.go

```
func setupMember(t *testing.T, members []*Membership) (
	[]*Membership, *handler,
) {
	id := len(members)
	ports := dynaport.Get(1)
	addr := fmt.Sprintf("%s:%d", "127.0.0.1", ports[0])
	tags := map[string]string{
		"rpc_addr": addr,
	}
	c := Config{
		NodeName: fmt.Sprintf("%d", id),
		BindAddr: addr,
		Tags:     tags,
	}
	h := &handler{}
	if len(members) == 0 {
		h.joins = make(chan map[string]string, 3)
		h.leaves = make(chan string, 3)
	} else {
		c.StartJoinAddrs = []string{
			members[0].BindAddr,
		}
	}
	m, err := New(h, c)
	require.NoError(t, err)
	members = append(members, m)
	return members, h
}
```

setupMember() sets up a new member under a free port and with the member's length as the node name so the names are unique. The member's length also tells us whether this member is the cluster's initial member or we have a cluster to join.

Define the handler mock and finish the test code by putting this snippet below setupMember():

ServerSideServiceDiscovery/internal/discovery/membership_test.go

```
type handler struct {
	joins  chan map[string]string
	leaves chan string
}

func (h *handler) Join(id, addr string) error {
	if h.joins != nil {
```

```
			h.joins <- map[string]string{
				"id":   id,
				"addr": addr,
			}
		}
		return nil
}

func (h *handler) Leave(id string) error {
		if h.leaves != nil {
			h.leaves <- id
		}
		return nil
}
```

The handler mock tracks how many times our Membership calls the handler's Join() and Leave() methods, and with what IDs and addresses.

Run the Membership's tests and verify they pass.

Now that we have our discovery and membership package, let's integrate it with our service and build something we couldn't before—replication!

Request Discovered Services and Replicate Logs

Let's build on our service discovery to add replication in our service so that we store multiple copies of the log data when we have multiple servers in a cluster. Replication makes our service more resilient to failures. For example, if a node's disk fails and we can't recover its data, replication can save our butts because it ensures that there's a copy saved on another disk.

In the next chapter, we'll coordinate the servers so our replication will have a defined leader-follower relationship, but for now we simply want the servers to replicate each other when they discover each other and not worry about whether they should, like the scientists from Jurassic Park. Our goal for the rest of this chapter is to build something simple that makes use of our service's discovery and sets us up for our coordinated replication in the next chapter.

Discovery alone isn't useful—so what if a bunch of computers discover each other and they just sit there doing nothing? Discovery is important because the discovery events trigger other processes in our service like replication and consensus. When servers discover other servers, we want to trigger the servers to replicate. We need a component in our service that handles when a server joins (or leaves) the cluster and begins (or ends) replicating from it.

Our replication will be pull-based, with the replication component consuming from each discovered server and producing a copy to the local server.

In pull-based replication, the consumer periodically polls the data source to check if it has new data to consume. In push-based replication, the data source pushes the data to its replicas. (In the next chapter we'll integrate Raft to our service—and it's push-based.)

Pull-based systems' flexibility can be great for log and message systems where the consumers and work loads can differ—for example, if you have a client that stream processes its data and runs continuously and you have a client that batch processes its data and runs every twenty-four hours. When replicating between servers, we replicate the newest data with as low latency as possible with homogeneous servers, so pull-based and push-based systems behave about the same. But it'll be easier to write our own pull-based replication that will highlight why we need consensus.

To add replication to our cluster, we need a replication component that acts as a membership handler handling when a server joins and leaves the cluster. When a server joins the cluster, the component will connect to the server and run a loop that consumes from the discovered server and produces to the local server.

In the internal/log directory, create a new file named replicator.go to contain our replication code, beginning with this snippet:

ServerSideServiceDiscovery/internal/log/replicator.go

```
package log

import (
	"context"
	"sync"

	"go.uber.org/zap"
	"google.golang.org/grpc"

	api "github.com/travisjeffery/proglog/api/v1"
)

type Replicator struct {
	DialOptions []grpc.DialOption
	LocalServer api.LogClient

	logger *zap.Logger

	mu      sync.Mutex
	servers map[string]chan struct{}
	closed  bool
	close   chan struct{}
}
```

The replicator connects to other servers with the gRPC client, and we need to configure the client so it can authenticate with the servers. The clientOptions field is how we pass in the options to configure the client. The servers field is a map of server addresses to a channel, which the replicator uses to stop replicating from a server when the server fails or leaves the cluster. The replicator calls the produce function to save a copy of the messages it consumes from the other servers.

Next, put the following Join() method below the replicator struct:

ServerSideServiceDiscovery/internal/log/replicator.go

```
func (r *Replicator) Join(name, addr string) error {
	r.mu.Lock()
	defer r.mu.Unlock()
	r.init()

	if r.closed {
		return nil
	}

	if _, ok := r.servers[name]; ok {
		// already replicating so skip
		return nil
	}
	r.servers[name] = make(chan struct{})

	go r.replicate(addr, r.servers[name])

	return nil
}
```

The Join(name, addr string) method adds the given server address to the list of servers to replicate and kicks off the add goroutine to run the actual replication logic.

Now put the replicate(addr string) method, containing the replication logic, below the previous snippet:

ServerSideServiceDiscovery/internal/log/replicator.go

```
func (r *Replicator) replicate(addr string, leave chan struct{}) {
	cc, err := grpc.Dial(addr, r.DialOptions...)
	if err != nil {
		r.logError(err, "failed to dial", addr)
		return
	}
	defer cc.Close()

	client := api.NewLogClient(cc)

	ctx := context.Background()
	stream, err := client.ConsumeStream(ctx,
		&api.ConsumeRequest{
			Offset: 0,
		},
	)
```

```
	if err != nil {
		r.logError(err, "failed to consume", addr)
		return
	}

	records := make(chan *api.Record)
	go func() {
		for {
			recv, err := stream.Recv()
			if err != nil {
				r.logError(err, "failed to receive", addr)
				return
			}
			records <- recv.Record
		}
	}()
```

You saw most of this code before when we tested our stream consumer and producer. Here we create a client and open up a stream to consume all logs on the server.

Append the following snippet to finish implementing replicate():

ServerSideServiceDiscovery/internal/log/replicator.go

```
	for {
		select {
		case <-r.close:
			return
		case <-leave:
			return
		case record := <-records:
			_, err = r.LocalServer.Produce(ctx,
				&api.ProduceRequest{
					Record: record,
				},
			)
			if err != nil {
				r.logError(err, "failed to produce", addr)
				return
			}
		}
	}
}
```

The loop consumes the logs from the discovered server in a stream and then produces to the local server to save a copy. We replicate messages from the other server until that server fails or leaves the cluster and the replicator closes the channel for that server, which breaks the loop and ends the replicate() goroutine. The replicator closes the channel when Serf receives an event saying that the other server left the cluster, and then this server calls the Leave() method that we're about to add.

Write the Leave(name string) method beneath your replicate() method with the following code:

ServerSideServiceDiscovery/internal/log/replicator.go
```
func (r *Replicator) Leave(name string) error {
	r.mu.Lock()
	defer r.mu.Unlock()
	r.init()
	if _, ok := r.servers[name]; !ok {
		return nil
	}
	close(r.servers[name])
	delete(r.servers, name)
	return nil
}
```

This Leave(name string) method handles the server leaving the cluster by removing the server from the list of servers to replicate and closes the server's associated channel. Closing the channel signals to the receiver in the replicate() goroutine to stop replicating from that server.

Next, add the following init() helper below your Leave() method:

ServerSideServiceDiscovery/internal/log/replicator.go
```
func (r *Replicator) init() {
	if r.logger == nil {
		r.logger = zap.L().Named("replicator")
	}
	if r.servers == nil {
		r.servers = make(map[string]chan struct{})
	}
	if r.close == nil {
		r.close = make(chan struct{})
	}
}
```

We use this init() helper to lazily initialize the server map. You should use lazy initialization to give your structs a useful zero value[2] because having a useful zero value reduces the API's size and complexity while maintaining the same functionality. Without a useful zero value, we'd either have to export a replicator constructor function for the user to call or export the servers field on the replicator struct for the user to set—making more API for the user to learn and then requiring them to write more code before they can use our struct.

---

2. https://dave.cheney.net/2013/01/19/what-is-the-zero-value-and-why-is-it-useful

Append the following snippet to implement the Close() method:

ServerSideServiceDiscovery/internal/log/replicator.go
```
func (r *Replicator) Close() error {
	r.mu.Lock()
	defer r.mu.Unlock()
	r.init()

	if r.closed {
		return nil
	}
	r.closed = true
	close(r.close)
	return nil
}
```

Close() closes the replicator so it doesn't replicate new servers that join the cluster and it stops replicating existing servers by causing the replicate() goroutines to return.

We have one last helper to add to handle errors. Add this logError(err error, msg, addr string) method at the bottom of the file:

ServerSideServiceDiscovery/internal/log/replicator.go
```
func (r *Replicator) logError(err error, msg, addr string) {
	r.logger.Error(
		msg,
		zap.String("addr", addr),
		zap.Error(err),
	)
}
```

With this method, we just log the errors because we have no other use for them and to keep the code short and simple. If your users need access to the errors, a technique you can use to expose these errors is to export an error channel and send the errors into it for your users to receive and handle.

That's it for our replicator. In terms of components, we now have our replicator, membership, log, and server. Each service instance must set up and connect these components together to work. For simpler, short-running programs, I'll make a run package that exports a Run() function that's responsible for running the program. Rob Pike's Ivy project[3] works this way. For more complex, long-running services, I'll make an agent package that exports an Agent type that manages the different components and processes

3. https://github.com/robpike/ivy

that make up the service. Hashicorp's Consul[4] works this way. Let's write an Agent for our service and then test our log, server, membership, and replicator end-to-end.

Create an internal/agent directory with a file named agent.go inside that begins with this code:

ServerSideServiceDiscovery/internal/agent/agent.go
```
package agent

import (
	"crypto/tls"
	"fmt"
	"net"
	"sync"

	"go.uber.org/zap"

	"google.golang.org/grpc"
	"google.golang.org/grpc/credentials"

	api "github.com/travisjeffery/proglog/api/v1"
	"github.com/travisjeffery/proglog/internal/auth"
	"github.com/travisjeffery/proglog/internal/discovery"
	"github.com/travisjeffery/proglog/internal/log"
	"github.com/travisjeffery/proglog/internal/server"
)

type Agent struct {
	Config

	log        *log.Log
	server     *grpc.Server
	membership *discovery.Membership
	replicator *log.Replicator

	shutdown     bool
	shutdowns    chan struct{}
	shutdownLock sync.Mutex
}
```

An Agent runs on every service instance, setting up and connecting all the different components. The struct references each component (log, server, membership, replicator) that the Agent manages.

After the Agent, add its Config struct:

ServerSideServiceDiscovery/internal/agent/agent.go
```
type Config struct {
	ServerTLSConfig *tls.Config
	PeerTLSConfig   *tls.Config
```

4. https://github.com/hashicorp/consul

```
        DataDir         string
        BindAddr        string
        RPCPort         int
        NodeName        string
        StartJoinAddrs  []string
        ACLModelFile    string
        ACLPolicyFile   string
}

func (c Config) RPCAddr() (string, error) {
        host, _, err := net.SplitHostPort(c.BindAddr)
        if err != nil {
                return "", err
        }
        return fmt.Sprintf("%s:%d", host, c.RPCPort), nil
}
```

The Agent sets up the components so its Config comprises the components' parameters to pass them through to the components.

Below Config, place this Agent creator function:

ServerSideServiceDiscovery/internal/agent/agent.go

```
func New(config Config) (*Agent, error) {
        a := &Agent{
                Config:    config,
                shutdowns: make(chan struct{}),
        }
        setup := []func() error{
                a.setupLogger,
                a.setupLog,
                a.setupServer,
                a.setupMembership,
        }
        for _, fn := range setup {
                if err := fn(); err != nil {
                        return nil, err
                }
        }
        return a, nil
}
```

New(Config) creates an Agent and runs a set of methods to set up and run the agent's components. After we run New(), we expect to have a running, functioning service. We've seen most of these setup codes before when testing our components, so we'll cover them quickly.

First, set up the logger with this setupLogger() method. Put setupLogger() under New():

ServerSideServiceDiscovery/internal/agent/agent.go

```
func (a *Agent) setupLogger() error {
	logger, err := zap.NewDevelopment()
	if err != nil {
		return err
	}
	zap.ReplaceGlobals(logger)
	return nil
}
```

Then, we set up the log with this setupLog() method. Put setupLog() under the previous snippet:

ServerSideServiceDiscovery/internal/agent/agent.go

```
func (a *Agent) setupLog() error {
	var err error
	a.log, err = log.NewLog(
		a.Config.DataDir,
		log.Config{},
	)
	return err
}
```

Now we set up the server with setupServer(). Add setupServer() after setupLog():

ServerSideServiceDiscovery/internal/agent/agent.go

```
func (a *Agent) setupServer() error {
	authorizer := auth.New(
		a.Config.ACLModelFile,
		a.Config.ACLPolicyFile,
	)
	serverConfig := &server.Config{
		CommitLog:  a.log,
		Authorizer: authorizer,
	}
	var opts []grpc.ServerOption
	if a.Config.ServerTLSConfig != nil {
		creds := credentials.NewTLS(a.Config.ServerTLSConfig)
		opts = append(opts, grpc.Creds(creds))
	}
	var err error
	a.server, err = server.NewGRPCServer(serverConfig, opts...)
	if err != nil {
		return err
	}
	rpcAddr, err := a.RPCAddr()
	if err != nil {
		return err
	}
```

```
	ln, err := net.Listen("tcp", rpcAddr)
	if err != nil {
		return err
	}
	go func() {
		if err := a.server.Serve(ln); err != nil {
			_ = a.Shutdown()
		}
	}()
	return err
}
```

Then we set up the membership with setupMembership(). Place setupMembership() after setupServer():

ServerSideServiceDiscovery/internal/agent/agent.go

```
func (a *Agent) setupMembership() error {
	rpcAddr, err := a.Config.RPCAddr()
	if err != nil {
		return err
	}
	var opts []grpc.DialOption
	if a.Config.PeerTLSConfig != nil {
		opts = append(opts, grpc.WithTransportCredentials(
			credentials.NewTLS(a.Config.PeerTLSConfig),
		),
		)
	}
	conn, err := grpc.Dial(rpcAddr, opts...)
	if err != nil {
		return err
	}
	client := api.NewLogClient(conn)
	a.replicator = &log.Replicator{
		DialOptions: opts,
		LocalServer: client,
	}
	a.membership, err = discovery.New(a.replicator, discovery.Config{
		NodeName: a.Config.NodeName,
		BindAddr: a.Config.BindAddr,
		Tags: map[string]string{
			"rpc_addr": rpcAddr,
		},
		StartJoinAddrs: a.Config.StartJoinAddrs,
	})
	return err
}
```

setupMembership() sets up a Replicator with the gRPC dial options needed to connect to other servers and a client so the replicator can connect to other servers, consume their data, and produce a copy of the data to the local server. Then we create a Membership passing in the replicator and its handler to notify the replicator when servers join and leave the cluster.

That's all of the agent's setup code. If we call New() now, we'd have a running agent. At some point we'll want to shut down the agent, so put this Shutdown() method at the bottom of the file:

ServerSideServiceDiscovery/internal/agent/agent.go

```
func (a *Agent) Shutdown() error {
	a.shutdownLock.Lock()
	defer a.shutdownLock.Unlock()
	if a.shutdown {
		return nil
	}
	a.shutdown = true
	close(a.shutdowns)

	shutdown := []func() error{
		a.membership.Leave,
		a.replicator.Close,
		func() error {
			a.server.GracefulStop()
			return nil
		},
		a.log.Close,
	}
	for _, fn := range shutdown {
		if err := fn(); err != nil {
			return err
		}
	}
	return nil
}
```

This ensures that the agent will shut down once even if people call Shutdown() multiple times. Then we shut down the agent and its components by:

- Leaving the membership so that other servers will see that this server has left the cluster and so that this server doesn't receive discovery events anymore;
- Closing the replicator so it doesn't continue to replicate;
- Gracefully stopping the server, which stops the server from accepting new connections and blocks until all the pending RPCs have finished; and
- Closing the log.

We've implemented Serf into our service, so we can now run multiple instances of our service that discover and then replicate each other's data. Let's write a test to check that our service discovery and replication works and to prevent us from introducing a regression when we build consensus in Chapter 8, Coordinate Your Services with Consensus, on page 141.

Test Discovery and the Service End-to-End

Let's test that our service discovery and replication works in an end-to-end test. We'll set up a cluster with three nodes. We'll produce a record to one server and verify that we can consume the message from the other servers that have (hopefully) replicated for us.

In internal/agent, create an agent_test.go file, beginning with this snippet:

ServerSideServiceDiscovery/internal/agent/agent_test.go
```go
package agent_test

import (
	"context"
	"crypto/tls"
	"fmt"
	"io/ioutil"
	"os"
	"testing"
	"time"

	"github.com/stretchr/testify/require"
	"github.com/travisjeffery/go-dynaport"
	"google.golang.org/grpc"
	"google.golang.org/grpc/credentials"

	api "github.com/travisjeffery/proglog/api/v1"
	"github.com/travisjeffery/proglog/internal/agent"
	"github.com/travisjeffery/proglog/internal/config"
)
```

What can I say? Our end-to-end test has a lot going on and requires a lot of imports to make it happen.

Now we can write the test beginning with this code:

ServerSideServiceDiscovery/internal/agent/agent_test.go
```go
func TestAgent(t *testing.T) {
	serverTLSConfig, err := config.SetupTLSConfig(config.TLSConfig{
		CertFile:      config.ServerCertFile,
		KeyFile:       config.ServerKeyFile,
		CAFile:        config.CAFile,
		Server:        true,
		ServerAddress: "127.0.0.1",
	})
```

```
        require.NoError(t, err)

        peerTLSConfig, err := config.SetupTLSConfig(config.TLSConfig{
                CertFile:      config.RootClientCertFile,
                KeyFile:       config.RootClientKeyFile,
                CAFile:        config.CAFile,
                Server:        false,
                ServerAddress: "127.0.0.1",
        })
        require.NoError(t, err)
```

This snippet defines the certificate configurations used in our test to test our security. The serverTLSConfig defines the configuration of the certificate that's served to clients. And the peerTLSConfig defines the configuration of the certificate that's served between servers so they can connect with and replicate each other.

Now set up the cluster by placing this code after the previous snippet:

ServerSideServiceDiscovery/internal/agent/agent_test.go

```
var agents []*agent.Agent
for i := 0; i < 3; i++ {
        ports := dynaport.Get(2)
        bindAddr := fmt.Sprintf("%s:%d", "127.0.0.1", ports[0])
        rpcPort := ports[1]

        dataDir, err := ioutil.TempDir("", "agent-test-log")
        require.NoError(t, err)

        var startJoinAddrs []string
        if i != 0 {
                startJoinAddrs = append(
                        startJoinAddrs,
                        agents[0].Config.BindAddr,
                )
        }

        agent, err := agent.New(agent.Config{
                NodeName:        fmt.Sprintf("%d", i),
                StartJoinAddrs:  startJoinAddrs,
                BindAddr:        bindAddr,
                RPCPort:         rpcPort,
                DataDir:         dataDir,
                ACLModelFile:    config.ACLModelFile,
                ACLPolicyFile:   config.ACLPolicyFile,
                ServerTLSConfig: serverTLSConfig,
                PeerTLSConfig:   peerTLSConfig,
        })
        require.NoError(t, err)

        agents = append(agents, agent)
}
defer func() {
```

```
        for _, agent := range agents {
                err := agent.Shutdown()
                require.NoError(t, err)
                require.NoError(t,
                        os.RemoveAll(agent.Config.DataDir),
                )
        }
}()
time.Sleep(3 * time.Second)
```

This code sets up a three-node cluster. The second and third nodes join the first node's cluster.

Because we now have two addresses to configure in our service (the RPC address and the Serf address), and because we run our tests on a single host, we need two ports. We used the 0 port trick in Test a gRPC Server and Client, on page 68, to get a port automatically assigned to a listener by net.Listen,[5] but now we just want the port—with no listener—so we use the dynaport library to allocate the two ports we need: one for our gRPC log connections and one for our Serf service discovery connections.

We defer a function call that runs after the test to verify that the agents successfully shut down and to delete the test data. We make the test sleep for a few seconds to give the nodes time to discover each other.

Now that we have a cluster, we can test it works. Put this code after the previous snippet:

ServerSideServiceDiscovery/internal/agent/agent_test.go

```
leaderClient := client(t, agents[0], peerTLSConfig)
produceResponse, err := leaderClient.Produce(
        context.Background(),
        &api.ProduceRequest{
                Record: &api.Record{
                        Value: []byte("foo"),
                },
        },
)
require.NoError(t, err)
consumeResponse, err := leaderClient.Consume(
        context.Background(),
        &api.ConsumeRequest{
                Offset: produceResponse.Offset,
        },
)
require.NoError(t, err)
require.Equal(t, consumeResponse.Record.Value, []byte("foo"))
```

5. https://golang.org/pkg/net/#Listen

This code is the same as our testProduceConsume() test case in Test a gRPC Server and Client, on page 68: it checks that we can produce to and consume from a single node. Now we need to check that another node replicated the record. We do that by adding this code to the test, below the previous snippet:

ServerSideServiceDiscovery/internal/agent/agent_test.go

```
	// wait until replication has finished
	time.Sleep(3 * time.Second)

	followerClient := client(t, agents[1], peerTLSConfig)
	consumeResponse, err = followerClient.Consume(
		context.Background(),
		&api.ConsumeRequest{
			Offset: produceResponse.Offset,
		},
	)
	require.NoError(t, err)
	require.Equal(t, consumeResponse.Record.Value, []byte("foo"))
}
```

Because our replication works asynchronously across servers, the logs produced to one server won't be immediately available on the replica servers. This process causes latency between when the message is produced to the first server and when it's replicated to the second. The stupid, simple[6] way to fix this (especially since we're black-box testing[7]) is to add a big enough delay in the test for the replicator to have replicated the message, but as small a delay as possible to keep our tests fast. Then we check that we can consume the replicated message.

Too Much Sleep Will Make Your Tests Too Slow

If we had enough test cases that needed a delay like this, eventually our tests would be slow and annoying to run, in which case we'd want to use a different technique. For example, you could retry your test's assertion in a loop with a small delay between iterations and timeout after a few seconds. Or you could have your server expose an event channel that included when the server produced a message. Then you'd wait to receive an event on that channel in your test so your test blocked and then continued the instant the second server replicated the message.

6. https://en.wikipedia.org/wiki/KISS_principle
7. https://en.wikipedia.org/wiki/Black-box_testing

Lastly, we need to add our client() helper that sets up a client for the service:

ServerSideServiceDiscovery/internal/agent/agent_test.go
```
func client(
	t *testing.T,
	agent *agent.Agent,
	tlsConfig *tls.Config,
) api.LogClient {
	tlsCreds := credentials.NewTLS(tlsConfig)
	opts := []grpc.DialOption{grpc.WithTransportCredentials(tlsCreds)}
	rpcAddr, err := agent.Config.RPCAddr()
	require.NoError(t, err)
	conn, err := grpc.Dial(fmt.Sprintf(
		"%s",
		rpcAddr,
	), opts...)
	require.NoError(t, err)
	client := api.NewLogClient(conn)
	return client
}
```

Now, run your tests with $ make test. If all is well, your tests pass and you've officially made a distributed service that can replicate data. Congrats!

What You Learned

Now when our servers discover other servers, they replicate each other's data. That's a problem with our replication implementation: when one server discovers another, they replicate each other in a cycle! You can verify it by adding this code at the bottom of your test:

```
consumeResponse, err = leaderClient.Consume(
 context.Background(),
 &api.ConsumeRequest{
  Offset: produceResponse.Offset + 1,
 },
)
require.Nil(t, consumeResponse)
require.Error(t, err)
got := grpc.Code(err)
want := grpc.Code(api.ErrOffsetOutOfRange{}.GRPCStatus().Err())
require.Equal(t, got, want)
```

We only produced one record to our service, and yet we're able to consume multiple records from the original server because it's replicated data from another server that replicated its data from the original server. No, Leo, we do not need to go deeper.

I mentioned that in the next chapter we'll work on coordinating the servers so that they'd have a defined leader-follower relationship so that only the followers would replicate the leader. We also want to control the *number* of replicas. Typically in a production deployment, three replicas is ideal: you could lose two and still not lose data, and with only three you won't be storing more data than necessary.

So let's work on building consensus with Raft and coordinating the nodes in our cluster.

CHAPTER 8

Coordinate Your Services with Consensus

Distributed services are like commercial kitchens. Imagine a small restaurant opens up with one stove and one cook. Patrons discover the restaurant and tell their friends, and business is booming. But the kitchen struggles with the mob of customers and sometimes the stove breaks, forcing the restaurant to close for the night and lose business. So the restaurant hires two more cooks and buys two more stoves. The cooks keep up with orders now but they make mistakes: they mix up appetizers and entrees; they mix up tables; they make double of one order while forgetting to make another. They lack coordination. So the kitchen hires a chef to oversee and coordinate the kitchen. When an order comes in, the chef divides the order and assigns the appetizers, entrees, and deserts to the cooks who prepare the food timely and correctly. The patrons love the fast, quality service, and the kitchen becomes world-renowned.

In this chapter, we look at the chef of distributed services: consensus. Consensus algorithms are tools used to get distributed services to agree on shared state even in the face of failures. In Request Discovered Services and Replicate Logs, on page 123, we naively implemented replication in our service, and the servers replicate each other in a cycle, making infinite copies of the same data. We need to put the servers in leader and follower relationships where the followers replicate the leader's data. We'll do just that in this chapter using Raft for leader election and replication.

What Is Raft and How Does It Work?

Raft is a distributed consensus algorithm designed to be easily understood and implemented. It's the consensus algorithm behind services like Etcd—the distributed key-value store that backs Kubernetes, Consul, and soon Kafka, whose team is migrating from ZooKeeper to Raft.[1] Because Raft is easy to understand and implement, developers have written many quality Raft libraries used in many projects and it's become the most widely deployed consensus algorithm today.

Let's talk about Raft's leader election first and then talk about its replication, and that'll transition into coding replication in our service.

Leader Election

A Raft cluster has one leader and the rest of the servers are followers. The leader maintains power by sending heartbeat requests to its followers, effectively saying: "I'm still here and I'm still the boss." If the follower times out waiting for a heartbeat request from the leader, then the follower becomes a candidate and begins an election to decide the next leader. The candidate votes for itself and then requests votes from the followers. "The boss is gone! I'm the new boss, right?" If the candidate receives a majority of the votes, it becomes the leader, and it sends heartbeat requests to the followers to establish authority: "Hey y'all, new boss here."

Followers can become candidates simultaneously if they time out at the same time waiting for the leader's heartbeats. They'll hold their own elections and the elections might not result in a new leader because of vote splitting. So they'll hold another election. Candidates will hold elections until there's a winner that becomes the new leader.

Every Raft server has a *term*: a monotonically increasing integer that tells other servers how authoritative and current this server is. The servers' terms act as a logical clock: a way to capture chronological and causal relationships in distributed systems, where real-time clocks are untrustworthy and unimportant. Each time a candidate begins an election, it increments its term. If the candidate wins the election and becomes the leader, the followers update their terms to match and the terms don't change until the next election. Servers vote once per term for the first candidate that requests votes, as long as the candidate's term is greater than the voters'. These conditions help prevent vote splits and ensure the voters elect an up-to-date leader.

Depending on your use case, you might use Raft just for leader election. Imagine you've built a job system with a database of jobs to run and a program that queries the database every second to check if there's a job to run and, if so, runs the job. You want this system to be highly available and resilient

1. https://cwiki.apache.org/confluence/display/KAFKA/KIP-500:+Replace+ZooKeeper+with+a+Self-Managed+Metadata+Quorum

to failures, so you run multiple instances of the job runner. But you don't want all of the runners running simultaneously and duplicating the work. So you use Raft to elect a leader; only the leader runs the jobs, and if the leader fails, Raft elects a new leader that runs the jobs. Most use cases rely on Raft for both its leader election and replication to get consensus on state.

Raft's leader election can be useful by itself, but usually the point is to elect a leader that's responsible for replicating a log to its followers and doing something with the log data. Raft breaks consensus into two parts: leader election and log replication. Let's talk about how Raft's replication works.

Log Replication

The leader accepts client requests, each of which represents some command to run across the cluster. (In a key-value service for example, you'd have a command to assign a key's value.) For each request, the leader appends the command to its log and then requests its followers to append the command to their logs. After a majority of followers have replicated the command—when the leader considers the command committed—the leader executes the command with a finite-state machine and responds to the client with the result. The leader tracks the highest committed offset and sends this in the requests to its followers. When a follower receives a request, it executes all commands up to the highest committed offset with its finite-state machine. All Raft servers run the same finite-state machine that defines how to handle each command.

Replication saves us from losing data when servers fail. There's a cost-benefit to replication. Like any insurance, replication costs (in complexity, in network bandwidth, in data storage), but the benefit of having replicated data to handle when a server fails makes it worth paying for the time the servers work. A Raft leader replicates to most of its followers, assuring that we won't lose data unless a majority of the followers fail.

The recommended number of servers in a Raft cluster is three and five. A Raft cluster of three servers will tolerate a single server failure while a cluster of five will tolerate two server failures. I recommend odd number cluster sizes because Raft will handle (N–1)/2 failures, where N is the size of your cluster. If you had a cluster with four servers, it would handle losing one server, the same as a cluster with three servers—so you'd pay for an extra server that didn't increase your fault tolerance. For larger clusters, CockRoachDB wrote a layer on top of Raft called MultiRaft[2] that divides the database's data into

2. https://www.cockroachlabs.com/blog/scaling-raft

ranges, each with its own consensus group. To keep our project simple, we'll have a single Raft cluster.

Our service's use case is unique because replicating a log is our end goal. Raft's algorithm replicates a log, and we could defer all log management to Raft's internals. This would make our service efficient and easy to code, but wouldn't teach you how to use Raft to build distributed services that aren't distributed logs.

In other services, you'll use Raft as a means to replicate a log of commands and then execute those commands with state machines. If you were building a distributed SQL database, you'd replicate and execute the insert and update SQL commands; if you were building a key-value store, you'd replicate and execute set commands. Because other services you build will replicate a log as a means rather than an end, we'll build our service the way you would other types of service, by replicating the transformation commands—which in our service are append commands. Technically we'll replicate two logs: the log containing Raft's commands and the log that results from the finite-state machines applying those commands. This service may not be as optimized as it could be, but what you'll learn will be more useful for when you build other services.

Implement Raft in Our Service

We have a log that can write and read records on one computer. We want a distributed log that's replicated on multiple computers, so let's implement Raft in our service to get that.

Install Raft by running this command:

```
$ go get github.com/hashicorp/raft@v1.1.1
$ # use etcd's fork of Ben Johnson's Bolt key/value store,
$ # which includes fixes for Go 1.14+
$ go mod edit -replace github.com/hashicorp/raft-boltdb=\
github.com/travisjeffery/raft-boltdb@v1.0.0
```

In the internal/log directory, create a distributed.go file, beginning with this snippet:

CoordinateWithConsensus/internal/log/distributed.go

```go
package log

import (
	"bytes"
	"crypto/tls"
	"fmt"
	"io"
	"net"
	"os"
```

```
	"path/filepath"
	"time"

	raftboltdb "github.com/hashicorp/raft-boltdb"
	"google.golang.org/protobuf/proto"

	"github.com/hashicorp/raft"

	api "github.com/travisjeffery/proglog/api/v1"
)

type DistributedLog struct {
	config Config
	log    *Log
	raft   *raft.Raft
}

func NewDistributedLog(dataDir string, config Config) (
	*DistributedLog,
	error,
) {
	l := &DistributedLog{
		config: config,
	}
	if err := l.setupLog(dataDir); err != nil {
		return nil, err
	}
	if err := l.setupRaft(dataDir); err != nil {
		return nil, err
	}
	return l, nil
}
```

This code defines our distributed log type and a function to create the log. The function defers the logic to the setup methods we'll write shortly. The log package will contain the single-server, non-replicated log we wrote earlier, and the distributed, replicated log built with Raft.

Write this setupLog() method under NewDistributedLog():

CoordinateWithConsensus/internal/log/distributed.go

```
func (l *DistributedLog) setupLog(dataDir string) error {
	logDir := filepath.Join(dataDir, "log")
	if err := os.MkdirAll(logDir, 0755); err != nil {
		return err
	}
	var err error
	l.log, err = NewLog(logDir, l.config)
	return err
}
```

setupLog(dataDir string) creates the log for this server, where this server will store the user's records.

Set Up Raft

A Raft instance comprises:

- A finite-state machine that applies the commands you give Raft;
- A log store where Raft stores those commands;
- A stable store where Raft stores the cluster's configuration—the servers in the cluster, their addresses, and so on;
- A snapshot store where Raft stores compact snapshots of its data; and
- A transport that Raft uses to connect with the server's peers.

We must set these up to create a Raft instance. Below setupLog(), add this setupRaft() method:

CoordinateWithConsensus/internal/log/distributed.go

```
func (l *DistributedLog) setupRaft(dataDir string) error {
	fsm := &fsm{log: l.log}

	logDir := filepath.Join(dataDir, "raft", "log")
	if err := os.MkdirAll(logDir, 0755); err != nil {
		return err
	}
	logConfig := l.config
	logConfig.Segment.InitialOffset = 1
	logStore, err := newLogStore(logDir, logConfig)
	if err != nil {
		return err
	}
```

setupRaft(dataDir string) configures and creates the server's Raft instance.

We begin by creating our finite-state machine (FSM) that we'll implement later in this file.

Then we create Raft's log store, and we use our own log we wrote in Code the Store, on page 26! We configure our log's initial offset to 1, as required by Raft. Raft needs a specific log interface satisfied, so we'll wrap our log to provide those APIs (we'll write that wrapper shortly):

CoordinateWithConsensus/internal/log/distributed.go

```
stableStore, err := raftboltdb.NewBoltStore(
	filepath.Join(dataDir, "raft", "stable"),
)
if err != nil {
	return err
}

retain := 1
```

```
snapshotStore, err := raft.NewFileSnapshotStore(
	filepath.Join(dataDir, "raft"),
	retain,
	os.Stderr,
)
if err != nil {
	return err
}

maxPool := 5
timeout := 10 * time.Second
transport := raft.NewNetworkTransport(
	l.config.Raft.StreamLayer,
	maxPool,
	timeout,
	os.Stderr,
)
```

The stable store is a key-value store where Raft stores important metadata, like the server's current term or the candidate the server voted for. Bolt[3] is an embedded and persisted key-value database for Go we've used as our stable store.

Then we set up Raft's snapshot store. Raft snapshots to recover and restore data efficiently, when necessary, like if your server's EC2 instance failed and an autoscaling group brought up another instance for the Raft server. Rather than streaming all the data from the Raft leader, the new server would restore from the snapshot (which you could store in S3 or a similar storage service) and then get the latest changes from the leader. This is more efficient and less taxing on the leader. You want to snapshot frequently to minimize the difference between the data in the snapshots and on the leader. The retain variable specifies that we'll keep one snapshot.

We create our transport that wraps a stream layer—a low-level stream abstraction (we'll write our own stream layer implementation in Stream Layer, on page 156):

CoordinateWithConsensus/internal/log/distributed.go

```
config := raft.DefaultConfig()
config.LocalID = l.config.Raft.LocalID
if l.config.Raft.HeartbeatTimeout != 0 {
	config.HeartbeatTimeout = l.config.Raft.HeartbeatTimeout
}
if l.config.Raft.ElectionTimeout != 0 {
	config.ElectionTimeout = l.config.Raft.ElectionTimeout
}
```

3. https://github.com/boltdb/bolt

```
if l.config.Raft.LeaderLeaseTimeout != 0 {
        config.LeaderLeaseTimeout = l.config.Raft.LeaderLeaseTimeout
}
if l.config.Raft.CommitTimeout != 0 {
        config.CommitTimeout = l.config.Raft.CommitTimeout
}
```

The config's LocalID field is the unique ID for this server, and it's the only config field we must set; the rest are optional, and in normal operation the default config should be fine.

To make our tests faster, we support overriding a handful of timeout configs to speed up Raft. For example, when we shut down the leader, we want the election to finish within a second, whereas in production you'd need a longer timeout to handle networking latency.

Add the following code to create the Raft instance and bootstrap the cluster:

CoordinateWithConsensus/internal/log/distributed.go

```
        l.raft, err = raft.NewRaft(
                config,
                fsm,
                logStore,
                stableStore,
                snapshotStore,
                transport,
        )
        if err != nil {
                return err
        }
        hasState, err := raft.HasExistingState(
                logStore,
                stableStore,
                snapshotStore,
        )
        if err != nil {
                return err
        }
        if l.config.Raft.Bootstrap && !hasState {
                config := raft.Configuration{
                        Servers: []raft.Server{{
                                ID:      config.LocalID,
                                Address: transport.LocalAddr(),
                        }},
                }
                err = l.raft.BootstrapCluster(config).Error()
        }
        return err
}
```

To support configuring Raft, add these highlighted lines to your log's Config struct in internal/log/config.go:

CoordinateWithConsensus/internal/log/config.go
```
package log

import (
	"github.com/hashicorp/raft"
)

type Config struct {
	Raft struct {
		raft.Config
		StreamLayer *StreamLayer
		Bootstrap   bool
	}
	Segment struct {
		MaxStoreBytes uint64
		MaxIndexBytes uint64
		InitialOffset uint64
	}
}
```

Generally you'll bootstrap a server configured with itself as the only voter, wait until it becomes the leader, and then tell the leader to add more servers to the cluster. The subsequently added servers don't bootstrap. That concludes our Raft setup. Let's continue building our DistributedLog.

Log API

We've written the code to set up a DistributedLog; next we'll write its public APIs that append records to and read records from the log and wrap Raft. The DistributedLog will have the same API as the Log type to make them interchangeable.

Add this Append() method below setupRaft():

CoordinateWithConsensus/internal/log/distributed.go
```
func (l *DistributedLog) Append(record *api.Record) (uint64, error) {
	res, err := l.apply(
		AppendRequestType,
		&api.ProduceRequest{Record: record},
	)
	if err != nil {
		return 0, err
	}
	return res.(*api.ProduceResponse).Offset, nil
}
```

Append(record *api.Record) appends the record to the log. Unlike in Code the Store, on page 26, where we appended the record directly to this server's log, we tell

Raft to apply a command (we've reused for the ProduceRequest for the command) that tells the FSM to append the record to the log. Raft runs the process described in Log Replication, on page 143, to replicate the command to a majority of the Raft servers and ultimately append the record to a majority of Raft servers.

Put this apply() method below Apply():

CoordinateWithConsensus/internal/log/distributed.go
```
func (l *DistributedLog) apply(reqType RequestType, req proto.Message) (
	interface{},
	error,
) {
	var buf bytes.Buffer
	_, err := buf.Write([]byte{byte(reqType)})
	if err != nil {
		return nil, err
	}
	b, err := proto.Marshal(req)
	if err != nil {
		return nil, err
	}
	_, err = buf.Write(b)
	if err != nil {
		return nil, err
	}
	timeout := 10 * time.Second
	future := l.raft.Apply(buf.Bytes(), timeout)
	if future.Error() != nil {
		return nil, future.Error()
	}
	res := future.Response()
	if err, ok := res.(error); ok {
		return nil, err
	}
	return res, nil
}
```

apply(reqType RequestType, req proto.Marshaler) wraps Raft's API to apply requests and return their responses. Even though we have only one request type, the append request type, I've written things that easily support multiple request types to show how you would set up your own services when you have different requests. In apply(), we marshal the request type and request into bytes that Raft uses as the record's data it replicates. The l.raft.Apply(buf.Bytes(), timeout) call has a lot going on behind the scenes, running the steps described in Log Replication, on page 143, to replicate the record and append the record to the leader's log.

The future.Error() API returns an error when something went wrong with Raft's replication. For example, it took too long for Raft to process the command or the server had to shutdown—the future.Error() API doesn't return your service's errors. The future.Response() API returns what your FSM's Apply() method returned and, opposed to Go's convention of using Go's multiple return values to separate errors, you must return a single value for Raft. In our apply() method we check whether the value is an error with a type assertion.

Put this Read() method below apply():

CoordinateWithConsensus/internal/log/distributed.go

```
func (l *DistributedLog) Read(offset uint64) (*api.Record, error) {
	return l.log.Read(offset)
}
```

Read(offset uint64) reads the record for the offset from the server's log. When you're okay with relaxed consistency, read operations need not go through Raft. When you need strong consistency, where reads must be up-to-date with writes, then you must go through Raft, but then reads are less efficient and take longer.

Finite-State Machine

Raft defers the running of your business logic to the FSM. After the previous snippet, define your fsm type with this code:

CoordinateWithConsensus/internal/log/distributed.go

```
var _ raft.FSM = (*fsm)(nil)

type fsm struct {
	log *Log
}
```

The FSM must access the data it manages. In our service, that's a log, and the FSM appends records to the log. If you were writing a key-value service, then your FSM would update the store of your data: an int, a map, Postgres —whatever store you've used.

Your FSM must implement three methods:

- Apply(record *raft.Log)—Raft invokes this method after committing a log entry.
- Snapshot()—Raft periodically calls this method to snapshot its state. For most services, you'll be able to build a compacted log—for example, if we were building a key-value store and we had a bunch of commands saying "set foo to bar," "set foo to baz," "set foo to qux," and so on, we would only set the latest command to restore the current state. Because we're replicating a log itself, we need the full log to restore it.

- Restore(io.ReadCloser)—Raft calls this to restore an FSM from a snapshot—for instance, if an EC2 instance failed and a new instance took its place.

Put this code below the fsm type to implement Apply():

CoordinateWithConsensus/internal/log/distributed.go
```
type RequestType uint8

const (
	AppendRequestType RequestType = 0
)

func (l *fsm) Apply(record *raft.Log) interface{} {
	buf := record.Data
	reqType := RequestType(buf[0])
	switch reqType {
	case AppendRequestType:
		return l.applyAppend(buf[1:])
	}
	return nil
}

func (l *fsm) applyAppend(b []byte) interface{} {
	var req api.ProduceRequest
	err := proto.Unmarshal(b, &req)
	if err != nil {
		return err
	}
	offset, err := l.log.Append(req.Record)
	if err != nil {
		return err
	}
	return &api.ProduceResponse{Offset: offset}
}
```

As I mentioned earlier, even though our service has only one command to replicate, I want to develop things to support multiple commands and show you how to do it for your own projects. So in this snippet, we make our own request type and define our append request type. When we send a request to Raft for it to apply, and when we read the request in the FSM's Apply() method to apply it, these request types identify the request and tell us how to handle it. In Apply(), we switch on the request type and call the corresponding method containing the logic to run the command. In applyAppend([]byte), we unmarshal the request and then append the record to the local log and return the response for Raft to send back to where we called raft.Apply() in DistributedLog.Append().

Below applyAppend(), put this snippet to support snapshots:

CoordinateWithConsensus/internal/log/distributed.go

```
func (f *fsm) Snapshot() (raft.FSMSnapshot, error) {
	r := f.log.Reader()
	return &snapshot{reader: r}, nil
}

var _ raft.FSMSnapshot = (*snapshot)(nil)

type snapshot struct {
	reader io.Reader
}

func (s *snapshot) Persist(sink raft.SnapshotSink) error {
	if _, err := io.Copy(sink, s.reader); err != nil {
		_ = sink.Cancel()
		return err
	}
	return sink.Close()
}

func (s *snapshot) Release() {}
```

Snapshot() returns an FSMSnapshot that represents a point-in-time snapshot of the FSM's state. In our case that state is our FSM's log, so call Reader() to return an io.Reader that will read all the log's data.

These snapshots serve two purposes: they allow Raft to compact its log so it doesn't store logs whose commands Raft has applied already. And they allow Raft to bootstrap new servers more efficiently than if the leader had to replicate its entire log again and again.

Raft calls Snapshot() according to your configured SnapshotInterval (how often Raft checks if it should snapshot—default is two minutes) and SnapshotThreshold (how many logs since the last snapshot before making a new snapshot—default is 8192).

Raft calls Persist() on the FSMSnapshot we created to write its state to some sink that, depending on the snapshot store you configured Raft with, could be in-memory, a file, an S3 bucket—something to store the bytes in. We're using the file snapshot store so that when the snapshot completes, we'll have a file containing all the Raft's log data. A shared state store such as S3 would put the burden of writing and reading the snapshot on S3 rather than the leader and allow new servers to restore snapshots without streaming from the leader. Raft calls Release() when it's finished with the snapshot.

Put this Restore() method below Release():

CoordinateWithConsensus/internal/log/distributed.go
```
func (f *fsm) Restore(r io.ReadCloser) error {
	b := make([]byte, lenWidth)
	var buf bytes.Buffer
	for i := 0; ; i++ {
		_, err := io.ReadFull(r, b)
		if err == io.EOF {
			break
		} else if err != nil {
			return err
		}
		size := int64(enc.Uint64(b))
		if _, err = io.CopyN(&buf, r, size); err != nil {
			return err
		}
		record := &api.Record{}
		if err = proto.Unmarshal(buf.Bytes(), record); err != nil {
			return err
		}
		if i == 0 {
			f.log.Config.Segment.InitialOffset = record.Offset
			if err := f.log.Reset(); err != nil {
				return err
			}
		}
		if _, err = f.log.Append(record); err != nil {
			return err
		}
		buf.Reset()
	}
	return nil
}
```

Raft calls Restore() to restore an FSM from a snapshot. For example, if we lost a server and scaled up a new one, we'd want to restore its FSM. The FSM must discard existing state to make sure its state will match the leader's replicated state.

In our Restore() implementation, we reset the log and configure its initial offset to the first record's offset we read from the snapshot so the log's offsets match. Then we read the records in the snapshot and append them to our new log.

That's it for our FSM code.

Next, put this snippet below the FSM to define Raft's log store:

CoordinateWithConsensus/internal/log/distributed.go
```
var _ raft.LogStore = (*logStore)(nil)
```

```
type logStore struct {
	*Log
}

func newLogStore(dir string, c Config) (*logStore, error) {
	log, err := NewLog(dir, c)
	if err != nil {
		return nil, err
	}
	return &logStore{log}, nil
}
```

Raft calls your FSM's Apply() method with *raft.Log's read from its managed log store. Raft replicates a log and then calls your state machine with the log's records. We're using our own log as Raft's log store, but we need to wrap our log to satisfy the LogStore interface Raft requires. In this snippet, we've defined our log store and a function to create it.

Below newLogStore() add this snippet:

CoordinateWithConsensus/internal/log/distributed.go

```
func (l *logStore) FirstIndex() (uint64, error) {
	return l.LowestOffset()
}

func (l *logStore) LastIndex() (uint64, error) {
	off, err := l.HighestOffset()
	return off, err
}

func (l *logStore) GetLog(index uint64, out *raft.Log) error {
	in, err := l.Read(index)
	if err != nil {
		return err
	}
	out.Data = in.Value
	out.Index = in.Offset
	out.Type = raft.LogType(in.Type)
	out.Term = in.Term
	return nil
}
```

Raft uses these APIs to get records and information about the log. We support the functionality on our log already and just needed to wrap our existing methods. What we call offsets, Raft calls indexes.

Put the following snippet below GetLog():

CoordinateWithConsensus/internal/log/distributed.go

```
func (l *logStore) StoreLog(record *raft.Log) error {
	return l.StoreLogs([]*raft.Log{record})
}
```

```
func (l *logStore) StoreLogs(records []*raft.Log) error {
	for _, record := range records {
		if _, err := l.Append(&api.Record{
			Value: record.Data,
			Term:  record.Term,
			Type:  uint32(record.Type),
		}); err != nil {
			return err
		}
	}
	return nil
}
```

Raft uses these APIs to append records to its log. Again, we just translate the call to our log's API and our record type. These changes require adding some fields to our Record type.

Change your Record message in api/v1/log.proto to the following:

CoordinateWithConsensus/api/v1/log.proto

```
message Record {
  bytes value = 1;
  uint64 offset = 2;
  uint64 term = 3;
  uint32 type = 4;
}
```

Then compile your protobuf by running $ make compile.

The last method on the logStore is a method to delete old records. Below StoreLogs(), put this DeleteRange() method:

CoordinateWithConsensus/internal/log/distributed.go

```
func (l *logStore) DeleteRange(min, max uint64) error {
	return l.Truncate(max)
}
```

DeleteRange(min, max uint64) removes the records between the offsets—it's to remove records that are old or stored in a snapshot.

Stream Layer

Raft uses a stream layer in the transport to provide a low-level stream abstraction to connect with Raft servers. Our stream layer must satisfy Raft's StreamLayer interface:

```
type StreamLayer interface {
 net.Listener
 // Dial is used to create a new outgoing connection
 Dial(address ServerAddress, timeout time.Duration) (net.Conn, error)
}
```

Add this snippet at the bottom of distributed.go to begin your StreamLayer:

CoordinateWithConsensus/internal/log/distributed.go
```
var _ raft.StreamLayer = (*StreamLayer)(nil)

type StreamLayer struct {
	ln              net.Listener
	serverTLSConfig *tls.Config
	peerTLSConfig   *tls.Config
}

func NewStreamLayer(
	ln net.Listener,
	serverTLSConfig,
	peerTLSConfig *tls.Config,
) *StreamLayer {
	return &StreamLayer{
		ln:              ln,
		serverTLSConfig: serverTLSConfig,
		peerTLSConfig:   peerTLSConfig,
	}
}
```

This snippet defines the StreamLayer type and checks that it satisfies the raft.StreamLayer interface. We want to enable encrypted communication between servers with TLS, so we need to take in the TLS configs used to accept incoming connections (the serverTLSConfig) and create outgoing connections (the peerTLSConfig).

Below NewStreamLayer(), add this Dial() method and RaftRPC constant:

CoordinateWithConsensus/internal/log/distributed.go
```
const RaftRPC = 1

func (s *StreamLayer) Dial(
	addr raft.ServerAddress,
	timeout time.Duration,
) (net.Conn, error) {
	dialer := &net.Dialer{Timeout: timeout}
	var conn, err = dialer.Dial("tcp", string(addr))
	if err != nil {
		return nil, err
	}
	// identify to mux this is a raft rpc
	_, err = conn.Write([]byte{byte(RaftRPC)})
	if err != nil {
		return nil, err
	}
	if s.peerTLSConfig != nil {
		conn = tls.Client(conn, s.peerTLSConfig)
	}
	return conn, err
}
```

Dial(addr raft.ServerAddress, timeout time.Duration) makes outgoing connections to other servers in the Raft cluster. When we connect to a server, we write the RaftRPC byte to identify the connection type so we can multiplex Raft on the same port as our Log gRPC requests. (We'll take a look at multiplexing shortly.) If we configure the stream layer with a peer TLS config, we make a TLS client-side connection.

The rest of the methods on the stream layer implement the net.Listener interface. Below Dial() add this snippet:

CoordinateWithConsensus/internal/log/distributed.go

```
func (s *StreamLayer) Accept() (net.Conn, error) {
	conn, err := s.ln.Accept()
	if err != nil {
		return nil, err
	}
	b := make([]byte, 1)
	_, err = conn.Read(b)
	if err != nil {
		return nil, err
	}
	if bytes.Compare([]byte{byte(RaftRPC)}, b) != 0 {
		return nil, fmt.Errorf("not a raft rpc")
	}
	if s.serverTLSConfig != nil {
		return tls.Server(conn, s.serverTLSConfig), nil
	}
	return conn, nil
}

func (s *StreamLayer) Close() error {
	return s.ln.Close()
}

func (s *StreamLayer) Addr() net.Addr {
	return s.ln.Addr()
}
```

Accept() is the mirror of Dial(). We accept the incoming connection and read the byte that identifies the connection and then create a server-side TLS connection. Close() closes the listener. Addr() returns the listener's address.

Discovery Integration

The next step to implement Raft in our service is to integrate our Serf-driven discovery layer with Raft to make the corresponding change in our Raft cluster when the Serf membership changes. Each time you add a server to the cluster, Serf will publish an event saying a member joined, and our discovery.Membership will call its handler's Join(id, addr string) method. When a server leaves the cluster, Serf will publish an event saying a member left, and our discovery.Membership will call its handler's Leave(id string) method. Our distributed log will act as our Membership's handler, so we need to implement those Join() and Leave() methods to update Raft.

Add this snippet below DistributedLog.Read(offset uint64) method:

CoordinateWithConsensus/internal/log/distributed.go

```
func (l *DistributedLog) Join(id, addr string) error {
	configFuture := l.raft.GetConfiguration()
	if err := configFuture.Error(); err != nil {
		return err
	}
	serverID := raft.ServerID(id)
	serverAddr := raft.ServerAddress(addr)
	for _, srv := range configFuture.Configuration().Servers {
		if srv.ID == serverID || srv.Address == serverAddr {
			if srv.ID == serverID && srv.Address == serverAddr {
				// server has already joined
				return nil
			}
			// remove the existing server
			removeFuture := l.raft.RemoveServer(serverID, 0, 0)
			if err := removeFuture.Error(); err != nil {
				return err
			}
		}
	}
	addFuture := l.raft.AddVoter(serverID, serverAddr, 0, 0)
	if err := addFuture.Error(); err != nil {
		return err
	}
	return nil
}

func (l *DistributedLog) Leave(id string) error {
	removeFuture := l.raft.RemoveServer(raft.ServerID(id), 0, 0)
	return removeFuture.Error()
}
```

Join(id, addr string) adds the server to the Raft cluster. We add every server as a voter, but Raft supports adding servers as non-voters with the AddNonVoter() API. You'd find non-voter servers useful if you wanted to replicate state to many servers to serve read only eventually consistent state. Each time you add more voter servers, you increase the probability that replications and elections will take longer because the leader has more servers it needs to communicate with to reach a majority.

Leave(id string) removes the server from the cluster. Removing the leader will trigger a new election.

Raft will error and return ErrNotLeader when you try to change the cluster on non-leader nodes. In our service discovery code we log all handler errors as critical, but if the node is a non-leader, then we should expect these errors and not log them. In internal/discovery/membership.go, import github.com/hashicorp/raft and update your logError() method to this:

CoordinateWithConsensus/internal/discovery/membership.go

```
func (m *Membership) logError(err error, msg string, member serf.Member) {
	log := m.logger.Error
	if err == raft.ErrNotLeader {
		log = m.logger.Debug
	}
	log(
		msg,
		zap.Error(err),
		zap.String("name", member.Name),
		zap.String("rpc_addr", member.Tags["rpc_addr"]),
	)
}
```

logError() will log the non-leader errors at the debug level now, and logs like these would be good candidates for removal.

Go back to internal/log/distributed.go and add this WaitForLeader() method below Leave():

CoordinateWithConsensus/internal/log/distributed.go

```
func (l *DistributedLog) WaitForLeader(timeout time.Duration) error {
	timeoutc := time.After(timeout)
	ticker := time.NewTicker(time.Second)
	defer ticker.Stop()
	for {
		select {
		case <-timeoutc:
			return fmt.Errorf("timed out")
		case <-ticker.C:
			if l := l.raft.Leader(); l != "" {
				return nil
			}
		}
	}
}
```

WaitForLeader(timeout time.Duration) blocks until the cluster has elected a leader or times out. It's useful when writing tests because, as we've discussed, most operations must run on the leader.

Put our last method on the DistributedLog under WaitForLeader():

CoordinateWithConsensus/internal/log/distributed.go
```
func (l *DistributedLog) Close() error {
	f := l.raft.Shutdown()
	if err := f.Error(); err != nil {
		return err
	}
	return l.log.Close()
}
```

Close() shuts down the Raft instance and closes the local log. And that wraps up the method on our DistributedLog. Now we'll build out the pieces that the distributed log and Raft depend on, beginning with the FSM.

Test the Distributed Log

Now let's test our distributed log. In the internal/log directory create a distributed_test.go file, beginning with this code:

CoordinateWithConsensus/internal/log/distributed_test.go
```
package log_test

import (
	"fmt"
	"io/ioutil"
	"net"
	"os"
	"reflect"
	"testing"
	"time"

	"github.com/hashicorp/raft"
	"github.com/stretchr/testify/require"
	"github.com/travisjeffery/go-dynaport"
	api "github.com/travisjeffery/proglog/api/v1"
	"github.com/travisjeffery/proglog/internal/log"
)

func TestMultipleNodes(t *testing.T) {
	var logs []*log.DistributedLog
	nodeCount := 3
	ports := dynaport.Get(nodeCount)

	for i := 0; i < nodeCount; i++ {
		dataDir, err := ioutil.TempDir("", "distributed-log-test")
		require.NoError(t, err)
		defer func(dir string) {
			_ = os.RemoveAll(dir)
		}(dataDir)
```

```
ln, err := net.Listen(
        "tcp",
        fmt.Sprintf("127.0.0.1:%d", ports[i]),
)
require.NoError(t, err)

config := log.Config{}
config.Raft.StreamLayer = log.NewStreamLayer(ln, nil, nil)
config.Raft.LocalID = raft.ServerID(fmt.Sprintf("%d", i))
config.Raft.HeartbeatTimeout = 50 * time.Millisecond
config.Raft.ElectionTimeout = 50 * time.Millisecond
config.Raft.LeaderLeaseTimeout = 50 * time.Millisecond
config.Raft.CommitTimeout = 5 * time.Millisecond
```

To begin TestMultipleServers(*testing.T), we set up a three-server cluster. We shorten the default Raft timeout configs so that Raft elects the leader quickly.

Below the previous code, add this snippet:

CoordinateWithConsensus/internal/log/distributed_test.go

```
        if i == 0 {
                config.Raft.Bootstrap = true
        }

        l, err := log.NewDistributedLog(dataDir, config)
        require.NoError(t, err)

        if i != 0 {
                err = logs[0].Join(
                        fmt.Sprintf("%d", i), ln.Addr().String(),
                )
                require.NoError(t, err)
        } else {
                err = l.WaitForLeader(3 * time.Second)
                require.NoError(t, err)
        }

        logs = append(logs, l)
}
```

The first server bootstraps the cluster, becomes the leader, and adds the other two servers to the cluster. The leader then must join other servers to its cluster.

Below the previous snippet, add this code:

CoordinateWithConsensus/internal/log/distributed_test.go

```
records := []*api.Record{
        {Value: []byte("first")},
        {Value: []byte("second")},
}
for _, record := range records {
        off, err := logs[0].Append(record)
        require.NoError(t, err)
```

```
        require.Eventually(t, func() bool {
                for j := 0; j < nodeCount; j++ {
                        got, err := logs[j].Read(off)
                        if err != nil {
                                return false
                        }
                        record.Offset = off
                        if !reflect.DeepEqual(got.Value, record.Value) {
                                return false
                        }
                }
                return true
        }, 500*time.Millisecond, 50*time.Millisecond)
}
```

We test our replication by appending some records to our leader server and check that Raft replicated the records to its followers. The Raft followers will apply the append message after a short latency, so we use testify's Eventually() method to give Raft enough time to finish replicating.

Now, finish the test by adding the following snippet:

CoordinateWithConsensus/internal/log/distributed_test.go

```
        err := logs[0].Leave("1")
        require.NoError(t, err)

        time.Sleep(50 * time.Millisecond)

        off, err := logs[0].Append(&api.Record{
                Value: []byte("third"),
        })
        require.NoError(t, err)

        time.Sleep(50 * time.Millisecond)

        record, err := logs[1].Read(off)
        require.IsType(t, api.ErrOffsetOutOfRange{}, err)
        require.Nil(t, record)

        record, err = logs[2].Read(off)
        require.NoError(t, err)
        require.Equal(t, []byte("third"), record.Value)
        require.Equal(t, off, record.Offset)
}
```

This code checks that the leader stops replicating to a server that's left the cluster, while continuing to replicate to the existing servers.

Multiplex to Run Multiple Services on One Port

Multiplexing allows you to serve different services on the same port. This makes your service easier to use: there's less documentation, less configuration, and fewer connections to manage. And you can serve multiple services even when a firewall constrains you to one port. There's a slight perf hit on each new connection because the multiplexer reads the first bytes to identify the connection, but for long-lived connections that performance hit is negligible. And you must be careful you don't accidentally expose a service.

Many distributed services that use Raft multiplex Raft with other services, like an RPC service. Running gRPC with mutual TLS makes multiplexing tricky because we want to multiplex the connection after the TLS handshake. Before the handshake, we can't differentiate the connections; we just know they're both TLS connections. We need to handshake and see the decrypted packets to know more. After the handshake, we can read the connection's packets to determine whether the connection is a gRPC or Raft connection. The issue with multiplexing mutual TLS gRPC connections is that gRPC needs information taken during the handshake to authenticate clients later on. So we have to multiplex before the handshake and need to make a way to identify Raft from gRPC connections.

We identify the Raft connections from the gRPC connections by making the Raft connections write a byte to identify them by. We write the number 1 as the first byte of our Raft connections to separate them from the gRPC connections. If we had other services, we could differentiate them from gRPC by passing a custom dialer to the gRPC client to send the number 2 as the first byte. The TLS standards[4] don't assign multiplexing schemes to the values 0–19, saying that they "require coordination," like we've done. It's better to handle internal services specially because you control the clients and can make them write whatever you need to identify them.

Let's update our agent to multiplex its Raft and gRPC connections and create a distributed log.

Update your imports in internal/agent/agent.go to the following:

CoordinateWithConsensus/internal/agent/agent.go

```
import (
	"bytes"
	"crypto/tls"
	"fmt"
	"io"
	"net"
	"sync"
	"time"
```

4. https://tools.ietf.org/html/rfc7983

```
	"go.uber.org/zap"
	"github.com/hashicorp/raft"
	"github.com/soheilhy/cmux"
	"google.golang.org/grpc"
	"google.golang.org/grpc/credentials"

	"github.com/travisjeffery/proglog/internal/auth"
	"github.com/travisjeffery/proglog/internal/discovery"
	"github.com/travisjeffery/proglog/internal/log"
	"github.com/travisjeffery/proglog/internal/server"
)
```

And then update your Agent type to this definition:

CoordinateWithConsensus/internal/agent/agent.go
```
type Agent struct {
	Config Config

	mux        cmux.CMux
	log        *log.DistributedLog
	server     *grpc.Server
	membership *discovery.Membership

	shutdown     bool
	shutdowns    chan struct{}
	shutdownLock sync.Mutex
}
```

Here we've added the mux cmux.CMux field, changed the log to a DistributedLog, and removed the replicator.

Add this field to your Config struct to enable bootstrapping the Raft cluster:

CoordinateWithConsensus/internal/agent/agent.go
```
Bootstrap bool
```

In the New() function, add the highlighted code to set up the mux (short for multiplexer):

CoordinateWithConsensus/internal/agent/agent.go
```
setup := []func() error {
	a.setupLogger,
	a.setupMux,
	a.setupLog,
	a.setupServer,
	a.setupMembership,
}
```

Then put setupMux() after the New() function:

CoordinateWithConsensus/internal/agent/agent.go
```
func (a *Agent) setupMux() error {
	rpcAddr := fmt.Sprintf(
		":%d",
		a.Config.RPCPort,
	)
	ln, err := net.Listen("tcp", rpcAddr)
	if err != nil {
		return err
	}
	a.mux = cmux.New(ln)
	return nil
}
```

setupMux() creates a listener on our RPC address that'll accept both Raft and gRPC connections and then creates the mux with the listener. The mux will accept connections on that listener and match connections based on your configured rules.

Let's update setupLog() to configure the rule to match Raft and create the distributed log. Replace your existing setupLog() method and put this snippet in its place:

CoordinateWithConsensus/internal/agent/agent.go
```
func (a *Agent) setupLog() error {
	raftLn := a.mux.Match(func(reader io.Reader) bool {
		b := make([]byte, 1)
		if _, err := reader.Read(b); err != nil {
			return false
		}
		return bytes.Compare(b, []byte{byte(log.RaftRPC)}) == 0
	})
```

In this snippet, we configure the mux that matches Raft connections. We identify Raft connections by reading one byte and checking that the byte matches the byte we set up our outgoing Raft connections to write in Stream Layer, on page 156:

CoordinateWithConsensus/internal/log/distributed.go
```
// identify to mux this is a raft rpc
_, err = conn.Write([]byte{byte(RaftRPC)})
if err != nil {
	return nil, err
}
```

If the mux matches this rule, it will pass the connection to the raftLn listener for Raft to handle the connection. Add the rest of setupLog() after the previous snippet:

CoordinateWithConsensus/internal/agent/agent.go
```
	logConfig := log.Config{}
	logConfig.Raft.StreamLayer = log.NewStreamLayer(
		raftLn,
		a.Config.ServerTLSConfig,
		a.Config.PeerTLSConfig,
	)
	logConfig.Raft.LocalID = raft.ServerID(a.Config.NodeName)
	logConfig.Raft.Bootstrap = a.Config.Bootstrap
	var err error
	a.log, err = log.NewDistributedLog(
		a.Config.DataDir,
		logConfig,
	)
	if err != nil {
		return err
	}
	if a.Config.Bootstrap {
		err = a.log.WaitForLeader(3 * time.Second)
	}
	return err
}
```

We configure the distributed log's Raft to use our multiplexed listener and then configure and create the distributed log.

Update your gRPC server to use the mux's listener by updating setupServer() to the following:

CoordinateWithConsensus/internal/agent/agent.go
```
func (a *Agent) setupServer() error {
	authorizer := auth.New(
		a.Config.ACLModelFile,
		a.Config.ACLPolicyFile,
	)
	serverConfig := &server.Config{
		CommitLog:  a.log,
		Authorizer: authorizer,
	}
	var opts []grpc.ServerOption
	if a.Config.ServerTLSConfig != nil {
		creds := credentials.NewTLS(a.Config.ServerTLSConfig)
		opts = append(opts, grpc.Creds(creds))
	}
	var err error
	a.server, err = server.NewGRPCServer(serverConfig, opts...)
	if err != nil {
		return err
	}
➤	grpcLn := a.mux.Match(cmux.Any())
➤	go func() {
```

```
                if err := a.server.Serve(grpcLn); err != nil {
                        _ = a.Shutdown()
                }
        }()
        return err
}
```

Because we've multiplexed two connection types (Raft and gRPC) and we added a matcher for the Raft connections, we know all other connections must be gRPC connections. We use cmux.Any() because it matches any connections. Then we tell our gRPC server to serve on the multiplexed listener.

Replace your setupMembership() method with the following:

CoordinateWithConsensus/internal/agent/agent.go

```
func (a *Agent) setupMembership() error {
        rpcAddr, err := a.Config.RPCAddr()
        if err != nil {
                return err
        }
        a.membership, err = discovery.New(a.log, discovery.Config{
                NodeName: a.Config.NodeName,
                BindAddr: a.Config.BindAddr,
                Tags: map[string]string{
                        "rpc_addr": rpcAddr,
                },
                StartJoinAddrs: a.Config.StartJoinAddrs,
        })
        return err
}
```

Our DistributedLog handles coordinated replication, thanks to Raft, so we don't need the Replicator anymore. Now we need the Membership to tell the DistributedLog when servers join or leave the cluster. Delete the a.replicator.Close line in Shutdown() and delete the internal/log/replicator.go file too. All that's left is to tell our mux to serve connections. Above the return statement in New(), add this line:

CoordinateWithConsensus/internal/agent/agent.go

```
go a.serve()
```

And then put serve() at the bottom of the file:

CoordinateWithConsensus/internal/agent/agent.go

```
func (a *Agent) serve() error {
        if err := a.mux.Serve(); err != nil {
                _ = a.Shutdown()
                return err
        }
        return nil
}
```

Now let's update our agent tests for Raft and test our replication and coordination. In What You Learned, on page 138, I showed you a test snippet that'd fail our test because our servers replicated each other in a cycle instead of adhering to a leader-follower relationship. That snippet will pass now!

In internal/agent/agent_test.go, add the following line to the agent's config:

CoordinateWithConsensus/internal/agent/agent_test.go
```
Bootstrap: i == 0,
```

This line is all we need to bootstrap the Raft cluster.

At the bottom of the test, add this snippet:

CoordinateWithConsensus/internal/agent/agent_test.go
```
consumeResponse, err = leaderClient.Consume(
	context.Background(),
	&api.ConsumeRequest{
		Offset: produceResponse.Offset + 1,
	},
)
require.Nil(t, consumeResponse)
require.Error(t, err)
got := grpc.Code(err)
want := grpc.Code(api.ErrOffsetOutOfRange{}.GRPCStatus().Err())
require.Equal(t, got, want)
```

Now we check that Raft has replicated the record we produced to the leader by consuming the record from a follower and that the replication stops there—the leader doesn't replicate from the followers.

Run your tests with $ make test. Your distributed service now uses Raft for consensus and replication!

What You Learned

In this chapter, you learned how to coordinate distributed services with Raft by adding leader election and replication to our service. We also looked at how to multiplex connections and run multiple services on one port. Next, we'll talk about client-side discovery, so clients can discover and call our servers.

CHAPTER 9

Discover Servers and Load Balance from the Client

We've gone through the belly of a whale and built a distributed service with discovery and consensus—a real distributed service! So far we've focused on the servers and haven't changed the clients beyond what gRPC gives us for free. In this chapter, we'll work on three client features that will improve our service's availability, scalability, and user experience. We'll enable our client to automatically:

- Discover servers in the cluster,
- Direct append calls to leaders and consume calls to followers, and
- Balance consume calls across followers.

After we've made these improvements, we'll be ready to deploy!

Three Load-Balancing Strategies

Three strategies can be used for solving the discovery and load balancing problem:

- *Server proxying*—your client sends its requests to a load balancer that knows the servers (either by querying a service registry or by being the service registry) and proxies the requests to your back-end services.

- *External load balancing*—your client queries an external load-balancing service that knows the servers and tells the client which server to send the RPC.

- *Client-side balancing*—your client queries a service registry to learn about the servers, picks the server to send its RPC, and sends its RPC directly to the server.

Using a server proxy is the most commonly used discovery and load-balancing pattern. Most servers don't trust their clients enough to give them control over how load balancing works because these decisions might affect the service's availability (for example, allowing a client to target a single server and call it until it's unavailable). You can put a proxy between clients and servers to act as a trust boundary. The proxy lets you control how your system ingests requests, as all the networking behind the proxy is in your network, trusted, and under your control. The server proxy knows about the servers it proxies to by maintaining or calling a service registry. People often use AWS's Elastic Load Balancer (ELB) to load balance external traffic from the internet. The ELB is an example of a service-side discovery router—incoming requests hit the ELB, and the ELB proxies that request to one instance registered with the ELB.

For complex and very accurate load balancing, you can run an external load balancer. The external load balancer knows all the servers and potentially all the clients, so it has all the data to decide the best server for the client to call. You pay for external load balancers with operational burden. I've never needed an external load balancer.

Alternatively, you can use client-side load balancing when you trust the clients. Client-side load balancing reduces latency and increases efficiency because requests go directly to their destination—there are no intermediates. This load balancing pattern is resilient because there isn't a single point of failure. However, you need to work on your network and security to give clients direct access to your servers.

We'll build client-side discovery and load balancing into our service because we control both the client and server and we designed our service for low-latency, high-throughput applications.

Load Balance on the Client in gRPC

Though the ideas we'll talk about in this chapter can apply to any client and server, because our service is a gRPC service, we'll use those terms. gRPC separates server discovery, load balancing, and client requests and response handling—often the only code you'll write is the latter. In gRPC, resolvers discover servers and pickers load balance by picking what server will handle the current request. gRPC also has balancers that manage subconnections but defer the load balancing to the pickers. gRPC provides an API (`base.NewBalancerBuilderV2`) to create a base balancer, but you probably won't have to write your own balancer.

When you call grpc.Dial, gRPC takes the address and passes it on to the resolver, and the resolver discovers the servers. gRPC's default resolver is the DNS resolver. If the address you give to gRPC has multiple DNS records associated with it, gRPC will balance the requests across each of those records' servers. You can write your own resolvers and use resolvers written by the community. For example, Kuberesolver[1] resolves the servers by fetching the endpoints from Kubernetes' API.

gRPC uses round-robin load balancing by default. The round-robin algorithm works by sending the first call to the first server, the second call to the second server, and so on. After the last server, it goes back to the first server again. So, we send each server the same number of calls. Round-robin works well when each request requires the same work by the server—stateless services that defer the work to a separate service like a database, for example. You can always begin with round-robin load balancing and optimize later.

The issue with round-robin load balancing, however, is that it doesn't consider what you know about each request, client, and server. For example:

- If your server is a replicated distributed service with a single writer and multiple readers, you'll want to read from replicas so the writer can focus on the writes. This requires knowing whether the request is a read or a write and whether the server is a primary or a replica.
- If your service is a globally distributed service, you'll want your clients to prioritize networking with local servers, which means you must know the location of the clients and the servers.
- If your system is latency sensitive, you can track metrics on how many in-flight or queued requests a server has or some other combination of latency metrics and have the client request the server with the smallest number.

Now you've seen how client-side discovery and load balancing work in gRPC, and when you might want to go beyond round-robin to load balance more efficiently, what can you do with this knowledge when building your own services?

The service we're building is a single-writer, multiple-reader distributed service—the leader server is the only server that can append to the log. Currently our clients connect to a single server, so if we want to call a leader and a follower, we have to create multiple clients. And if we want to balance consume calls across the followers, we have to manage it in our client code.

---

1. https://github.com/sercand/kuberesolver

We can solve some problems by writing our own resolver and picker: the resolver discovers the servers and what server is the leader, and the picker manages directing produce calls to the leader and balancing consume calls across the followers. The resolver and picker will make your service easier to use, and we'll be able to delete some of our test code too. Hopefully that sounds sweet to you—it does to me—so let's get started.

Make Servers Discoverable

Our resolver will need a way to discover the cluster's servers. It needs to know each server's address and whether or not it is the leader. In Implement Raft in Our Service, on page 144, we built Raft into our service, which knows the cluster's server and what server is the leader. We can expose this information to the resolver with an endpoint on our gRPC service.

Using an RPC for discovery will be easy because we built Serf and Raft into our service already. Kafka clients discover the cluster's brokers by requesting a metadata endpoint. Kafka's metadata endpoint responds with data that's stored and coordinated with ZooKeeper, though the Kafka developers plan to remove the dependency on ZooKeeper and build Raft into Kafka to coordinate this data, similar to our service. This will be a big change in how this data works in Kafka, specifically with how it manages what servers are in the cluster and how it elects leaders; however, little to nothing will have to change with how the clients discover the servers, thus showing the benefit of using a service endpoint for client-side discovery.

Open the `api/v1/log.proto` file and update the `Log` service to include the `GetServers()` endpoint like so:

ClientSideServiceDiscovery/api/v1/log.proto
```
service Log {
  rpc Produce(ProduceRequest) returns (ProduceResponse) {}
  rpc Consume(ConsumeRequest) returns (ConsumeResponse) {}
  rpc ConsumeStream(ConsumeRequest) returns (stream ConsumeResponse) {}
  rpc ProduceStream(stream ProduceRequest) returns (stream ProduceResponse)
    {}
  rpc GetServers(GetServersRequest) returns (GetServersResponse) {}
}
```

This is the endpoint resolvers will call to get the cluster's servers.

Now, add this snippet to the end of the file to define the endpoint's request and response:

ClientSideServiceDiscovery/api/v1/log.proto
```
message GetServersRequest {}
```

```
message GetServersResponse {
  repeated Server servers = 1;
}

message Server {
  string id = 1;
  string rpc_addr = 2;
  bool is_leader = 3;
}
```

The endpoint response includes the server addresses clients should connect to and what server is the leader. This information will tell the picker what server to send the server produce calls and what servers to send consume calls.

We'll implement the endpoint on our server, but before we do, we need an API on our DistributedLog that exposes Raft's server data. Open internal/log/distributed.go and put this GetServers() method below DistributedLog.Close:

ClientSideServiceDiscovery/internal/log/distributed.go

```
func (l *DistributedLog) GetServers() ([]*api.Server, error) {
	future := l.raft.GetConfiguration()
	if err := future.Error(); err != nil {
		return nil, err
	}
	var servers []*api.Server
	for _, server := range future.Configuration().Servers {
		servers = append(servers, &api.Server{
			Id:       string(server.ID),
			RpcAddr:  string(server.Address),
			IsLeader: l.raft.Leader() == server.Address,
		})
	}
	return servers, nil
}
```

Raft's configuration comprises the servers in the cluster and includes each server's ID, address, and suffrage—whether the server votes in Raft elections (we don't need the suffrage in our project). Raft can tell us the address of the cluster's leader, too. GetServers() converts the data from Raft's raft.Server type into our *api.Server type for our API to respond with.

Let's update the DistributedLog tests to check that GetServers() returns the servers in the cluster as we expect. Open internal/log/distributed_test.go and add the new code in this snippet that surrounds the old lines 8 and 9:

ClientSideServiceDiscovery/internal/log/distributed_test.go

```
Line 1 servers, err := logs[0].GetServers()
     - require.NoError(t, err)
     - require.Equal(t, 3, len(servers))
     - require.True(t, servers[0].IsLeader)
```

```
5  require.False(t, servers[1].IsLeader)
6  require.False(t, servers[2].IsLeader)
7
8  err = logs[0].Leave("1")
9  require.NoError(t, err)
10
11 time.Sleep(50 * time.Millisecond)
12
13 servers, err = logs[0].GetServers()
14 require.NoError(t, err)
15 require.Equal(t, 2, len(servers))
16 require.True(t, servers[0].IsLeader)
17 require.False(t, servers[1].IsLeader)
```

The assertions before line 8 test that GetServers() returns all three servers in the cluster and sets the leader server as the leader. After line 9, we expect the cluster to have two servers because these assertions run after we've made one server leave the cluster.

That's it for the DistributedLog changes and tests. Next we'll implement the endpoint on the server that calls DistributedLog.GetServers().

Open internal/server/server.go and update the Config to:

ClientSideServiceDiscovery/internal/server/server.go

```go
type Config struct {
	CommitLog   CommitLog
	Authorizer  Authorizer
	GetServerer GetServerer
}
```

And put this snippet below the ConsumeStream() method:

ClientSideServiceDiscovery/internal/server/server.go

```go
func (s *grpcServer) GetServers(
	ctx context.Context, req *api.GetServersRequest,
) (
	*api.GetServersResponse, error) {
	servers, err := s.GetServerer.GetServers()
	if err != nil {
		return nil, err
	}
	return &api.GetServersResponse{Servers: servers}, nil
}

type GetServerer interface {
	GetServers() ([]*api.Server, error)
}
```

These two snippets enable us to inject different structs that can get servers. We don't want to add the GetServers() method to our CommitLog interface because a non-distributed log like our Log type doesn't know about servers. So we made a new interface whose sole method GetServers() matches DistributedLog.GetServers. When we update the end-to-end tests in the agent package, we'll set our DistributedLog on the config as both the CommitLog and the GetServerer—which our new server endpoint wraps with error handling.

In agent.go, update your setupServer() method to configure the server to get the cluster's servers from the DistributedLog:

ClientSideServiceDiscovery/internal/agent/agent.go
```
serverConfig := &server.Config{
	CommitLog:   a.log,
	Authorizer:  authorizer,
	GetServerer: a.log,
}
```

Now we have a server endpoint that clients can call to get the cluster's servers. We're now ready to build our resolver.

Resolve the Servers

The gRPC resolver we'll write in this section will call the GetServers() endpoint we made and pass its information to gRPC so that the picker knows what servers it can route requests to.

To start, create a new package for our resolver and picker code by running $ mkdir internal/loadbalance.

gRPC uses the builder pattern for resolvers and pickers, so each has a builder interface and an implementation interface. Because the builder interfaces have one simple method—Build()—we'll implement both interfaces with one type. Create a file named resolver.go in internal/loadbalance that begins with this code:

ClientSideServiceDiscovery/internal/loadbalance/resolver.go
```
package loadbalance

import (
	"context"
	"fmt"
	"sync"

	"go.uber.org/zap"
	"google.golang.org/grpc"
	"google.golang.org/grpc/attributes"
	"google.golang.org/grpc/resolver"
	"google.golang.org/grpc/serviceconfig"

	api "github.com/travisjeffery/proglog/api/v1"
)
```

```
type Resolver struct {
        mu            sync.Mutex
        clientConn    resolver.ClientConn
        resolverConn  *grpc.ClientConn
        serviceConfig *serviceconfig.ParseResult
        logger        *zap.Logger
}
```

Resolver is the type we'll implement into gRPC's resolver.Builder and resolver.Resolver interfaces. The clientConn connection is the user's client connection and gRPC passes it to the resolver for the resolver to update with the servers it discovers. The resolverConn is the resolver's own client connection to the server so it can call GetServers() and get the servers.

Add this snippet below the Resolver type to implement gRPC's resolver.Builder interface:

ClientSideServiceDiscovery/internal/loadbalance/resolver.go

```
var _ resolver.Builder = (*Resolver)(nil)

func (r *Resolver) Build(
        target resolver.Target,
        cc resolver.ClientConn,
        opts resolver.BuildOptions,
) (resolver.Resolver, error) {
        r.logger = zap.L().Named("resolver")
        r.clientConn = cc
        var dialOpts []grpc.DialOption
        if opts.DialCreds != nil {
                dialOpts = append(
                        dialOpts,
                        grpc.WithTransportCredentials(opts.DialCreds),
                )
        }
        r.serviceConfig = r.clientConn.ParseServiceConfig(
                fmt.Sprintf(`{"loadBalancingConfig":[{"%s":{}}]}`, Name),
        )
        var err error
        r.resolverConn, err = grpc.Dial(target.Endpoint, dialOpts...)
        if err != nil {
                return nil, err
        }
        r.ResolveNow(resolver.ResolveNowOptions{})
        return r, nil
}

const Name = "proglog"

func (r *Resolver) Scheme() string {
        return Name
}
```

```
func init() {
	resolver.Register(&Resolver{})
}
```

resolver.Builder comprises two methods—Build() and Scheme():

- Build() receives the data needed to build a resolver that can discover the servers (like the target address) and the client connection the resolver will update with the servers it discovers. Build() sets up a client connection to our server so the resolver can call the GetServers() API.

- Scheme() returns the resolver's scheme identifier. When you call grpc.Dial, gRPC parses out the scheme from the target address you gave it and tries to find a resolver that matches, defaulting to its DNS resolver. For our resolver, you'll format the target address like this: proglog://your-service-address.

We register this resolver with gRPC in init() so gRPC knows about this resolver when it's looking for resolvers that match the target's scheme.

Put this snippet below init() to implement gRPC's resolver.Resolver interface:

ClientSideServiceDiscovery/internal/loadbalance/resolver.go

```
var _ resolver.Resolver = (*Resolver)(nil)

func (r *Resolver) ResolveNow(resolver.ResolveNowOptions) {
	r.mu.Lock()
	defer r.mu.Unlock()
	client := api.NewLogClient(r.resolverConn)
	// get cluster and then set on cc attributes
	ctx := context.Background()
	res, err := client.GetServers(ctx, &api.GetServersRequest{})
	if err != nil {
		r.logger.Error(
			"failed to resolve server",
			zap.Error(err),
		)
		return
	}
	var addrs []resolver.Address
	for _, server := range res.Servers {
		addrs = append(addrs, resolver.Address{
			Addr: server.RpcAddr,
			Attributes: attributes.New(
				"is_leader",
				server.IsLeader,
			),
		})
	}
```

```
		r.clientConn.UpdateState(resolver.State{
			Addresses:     addrs,
			ServiceConfig: r.serviceConfig,
		})
}

func (r *Resolver) Close() {
		if err := r.resolverConn.Close(); err != nil {
			r.logger.Error(
				"failed to close conn",
				zap.Error(err),
			)
		}
}
```

resolver.Resolver comprises two methods—ResolveNow() and Close(). gRPC calls ResolveNow() to resolve the target, discover the servers, and update the client connection with the servers. How your resolver will discover the servers depends on your resolver and the service you're working with. For example, a resolver built for Kubernetes could call Kubernetes' API to get the list of endpoints. We create a gRPC client for our service and call the GetServers() API to get the cluster's servers.

Services can specify how clients should balance their calls to the service by updating the state with a service config. We update the state with a service config that specifies to use the "proglog" load balancer we'll write in Route and Balance Requests with Pickers, on page 183.

You update the state with a slice of resolver.Address to inform the load balancer what servers it can choose from. A resolver.Address has three fields:

- Addr (required)—the address of the server to connect to.
- Attributes (optional but useful)—a map containing any data that's useful for the load balancer. We'll tell the picker what server is the leader and what servers are followers with this field.
- ServerName (optional and you likely don't need to set)—the name used as the transport certificate authority for the address, instead of the hostname taken from the Dial target string.

After we've discovered the servers, we update the client connection by calling UpdateState() with the resolver.Address's. We set up the addresses with the data in the api.Server's. gRPC may call ResolveNow() concurrently, so we use a mutex to protect access across goroutines.

Close() closes the resolver. In our resolver, we close the connection to our server created in Build().

That's it for our resolver's code. Let's test it.

Create a test file named resolver_test.go in internal/loadbalance that begins with this snippet:

ClientSideServiceDiscovery/internal/loadbalance/resolver_test.go

```
1  package loadbalance_test
2  
3  import (
4  	"net"
5  	"testing"
6  
7  	"github.com/stretchr/testify/require"
8  	"google.golang.org/grpc"
9  	"google.golang.org/grpc/attributes"
10 	"google.golang.org/grpc/credentials"
11 	"google.golang.org/grpc/resolver"
12 	"google.golang.org/grpc/serviceconfig"
13 
14 	api "github.com/travisjeffery/proglog/api/v1"
15 	"github.com/travisjeffery/proglog/internal/loadbalance"
16 	"github.com/travisjeffery/proglog/internal/config"
17 	"github.com/travisjeffery/proglog/internal/server"
18 )
19 
20 func TestResolver(t *testing.T) {
21 	l, err := net.Listen("tcp", "127.0.0.1:0")
22 	require.NoError(t, err)
23 
24 	tlsConfig, err := config.SetupTLSConfig(config.TLSConfig{
25 		CertFile:      config.ServerCertFile,
26 		KeyFile:       config.ServerKeyFile,
27 		CAFile:        config.CAFile,
28 		Server:        true,
29 		ServerAddress: "127.0.0.1",
30 	})
31 	require.NoError(t, err)
32 	serverCreds := credentials.NewTLS(tlsConfig)
33 
34 	srv, err := server.NewGRPCServer(&server.Config{
35 		GetServerer: &getServers{},
36 	}, grpc.Creds(serverCreds))
37 	require.NoError(t, err)
38 
39 	go srv.Serve(l)
```

This code sets up a server for our test resolver to try and discover some servers from. We pass in a mock GetServerers on line 35 so we can set what servers the resolver should find.

Put this snippet below the previous snippet to continue writing the test:

ClientSideServiceDiscovery/internal/loadbalance/resolver_test.go

```
conn := &clientConn{}
tlsConfig, err = config.SetupTLSConfig(config.TLSConfig{
	CertFile:      config.RootClientCertFile,
	KeyFile:       config.RootClientKeyFile,
	CAFile:        config.CAFile,
	Server:        false,
	ServerAddress: "127.0.0.1",
})
require.NoError(t, err)
clientCreds := credentials.NewTLS(tlsConfig)
opts := resolver.BuildOptions{
	DialCreds: clientCreds,
}
r := &loadbalance.Resolver{}
_, err = r.Build(
	resolver.Target{
		Endpoint: l.Addr().String(),
	},
	conn,
	opts,
)
require.NoError(t, err)
```

This code creates and builds the test resolver and configures its target endpoint to point to the server we set up in the previous snippet. The resolver will call GetServers() to resolve the servers and update the client connection with the servers' addresses.

Add this snippet below the previous snippet to finish writing the test:

ClientSideServiceDiscovery/internal/loadbalance/resolver_test.go

```
	wantState := resolver.State{
		Addresses: []resolver.Address{{
			Addr:       "localhost:9001",
			Attributes: attributes.New("is_leader", true),
		}, {
			Addr:       "localhost:9002",
			Attributes: attributes.New("is_leader", false),
		}},
	}
	require.Equal(t, wantState, conn.state)

	conn.state.Addresses = nil
	r.ResolveNow(resolver.ResolveNowOptions{})
	require.Equal(t, wantState, conn.state)
}
```

We check that the resolver updated the client connection with the servers and data we expected. We wanted the resolver to find two servers and mark the 9001 server as the leader.

Our test depended on some mock types. Add this code at the bottom of the file:

ClientSideServiceDiscovery/internal/loadbalance/resolver_test.go

```
type getServers struct{}

func (s *getServers) GetServers() ([]*api.Server, error) {
	return []*api.Server{{
		Id:       "leader",
		RpcAddr:  "localhost:9001",
		IsLeader: true,
	}, {
		Id:      "follower",
		RpcAddr: "localhost:9002",
	}}, nil
}

type clientConn struct {
	resolver.ClientConn
	state resolver.State
}

func (c *clientConn) UpdateState(state resolver.State) {
	c.state = state
}

func (c *clientConn) ReportError(err error) {}

func (c *clientConn) NewAddress(addrs []resolver.Address) {}

func (c *clientConn) NewServiceConfig(config string) {}

func (c *clientConn) ParseServiceConfig(
	config string,
) *serviceconfig.ParseResult {
	return nil
}
```

getServers implements GetServerers, whose job is to return a known server set for the resolver to find. clientConn implements resolver.ClientConn, and its job is to keep a reference to the state the resolver updated it with so that we can verify that the resolver updates the client connection with the correct data.

Run the resolver tests to verify that they pass. And now, we're on to the picker.

Route and Balance Requests with Pickers

In the gRPC architecture, pickers handle the RPC balancing logic. They're called *pickers* because they pick a server from the servers discovered by the resolver to handle each RPC. Pickers can route RPCs based on information about the RPC, client, and server, so their utility goes beyond balancing to any kind of request-routing logic.

To implement the picker builder, create a file named picker.go in internal/loadbalance that begins with this code:

ClientSideServiceDiscovery/internal/loadbalance/picker.go
```
package loadbalance

import (
	"strings"
	"sync"
	"sync/atomic"

	"google.golang.org/grpc/balancer"
	"google.golang.org/grpc/balancer/base"
)

var _ base.PickerBuilder = (*Picker)(nil)

type Picker struct {
	mu        sync.RWMutex
	leader    balancer.SubConn
	followers []balancer.SubConn
	current   uint64
}

func (p *Picker) Build(buildInfo base.PickerBuildInfo) balancer.Picker {
	p.mu.Lock()
	defer p.mu.Unlock()
	var followers []balancer.SubConn
	for sc, scInfo := range buildInfo.ReadySCs {
		isLeader := scInfo.
			Address.
			Attributes.
			Value("is_leader").(bool)
		if isLeader {
			p.leader = sc
			continue
		}
		followers = append(followers, sc)
	}
	p.followers = followers
	return p
}
```

Pickers use the builder pattern just like resolvers. gRPC passes a map of subconnections with information about those subconnections to Build() to set up the picker—behind the scenes, gRPC connected to the addresses that our resolver discovered. Our picker will route consume RPCs to follower servers and produce RPCs to the leader server. The address attributes help us differentiate the servers.

To implement the picker, add this snippet below Build():

ClientSideServiceDiscovery/internal/loadbalance/picker.go
```
var _ balancer.Picker = (*Picker)(nil)

func (p *Picker) Pick(info balancer.PickInfo) (
	balancer.PickResult, error) {
	p.mu.RLock()
	defer p.mu.RUnlock()
	var result balancer.PickResult
	if strings.Contains(info.FullMethodName, "Produce") ||
		len(p.followers) == 0 {
		result.SubConn = p.leader
	} else if strings.Contains(info.FullMethodName, "Consume") {
		result.SubConn = p.nextFollower()
	}
	if result.SubConn == nil {
		return result, balancer.ErrNoSubConnAvailable
	}
	return result, nil
}

func (p *Picker) nextFollower() balancer.SubConn {
	cur := atomic.AddUint64(&p.current, uint64(1))
	len := uint64(len(p.followers))
	idx := int(cur % len)
	return p.followers[idx]
}
```

Pickers have one method: Pick(balancer.PickInfo). gRPC gives Pick() a balancer.PickInfo containing the RPC's name and context to help the picker know what subconnection to pick. If you have header metadata, you can read it from the context. Pick() returns a balancer.PickResult with the subconnection to handle the call. Optionally, you can set a Done callback on the result that gRPC calls when the RPC completes. The callback tells you the RPC's error, trailer metadata, and whether there were bytes sent and received to and from the server.

We look at the RPC's method name to know whether the call is an append or consume call, and if we should pick a leader subconnection or a follower subconnection. We balance the consume calls across the followers with the round-robin algorithm. Put this snippet at the end of the file to register the picker with gRPC and finish the picker's code:

ClientSideServiceDiscovery/internal/loadbalance/picker.go
```
func init() {
	balancer.Register(
		base.NewBalancerBuilder(Name, &Picker{}, base.Config{}),
	)
}
```

Though pickers handle routing the calls, which we'd traditionally consider handling the balancing, gRPC has a balancer type that takes input from gRPC, manages subconnections, and collects and aggregates connectivity states. gRPC provides a base balancer; you probably don't need to write your own.

Time to test our picker. Create a test file named picker_test.go in internal/loadbalance that begins with this snippet:

ClientSideServiceDiscovery/internal/loadbalance/picker_test.go

```
package loadbalance_test

import (
	"testing"

	"google.golang.org/grpc/attributes"
	"google.golang.org/grpc/balancer"
	"google.golang.org/grpc/balancer/base"
	"google.golang.org/grpc/resolver"

	"github.com/stretchr/testify/require"

	"github.com/travisjeffery/proglog/internal/loadbalance"
)

func TestPickerNoSubConnAvailable(t *testing.T) {
	picker := &loadbalance.Picker{}
	for _, method := range []string{
		"/log.vX.Log/Produce",
		"/log.vX.Log/Consume",
	} {
		info := balancer.PickInfo{
			FullMethodName: method,
		}
		result, err := picker.Pick(info)
		require.Equal(t, balancer.ErrNoSubConnAvailable, err)
		require.Nil(t, result.SubConn)
	}
}
```

TestPickerNoSubConnAvailable() tests that a picker initially returns balancer.ErrNoSubConnAvailable before the resolver has discovered servers and updated the picker's state with available subconnections. balancer.ErrNoSubConnAvailable instructs gRPC to block the client's RPCs until the picker has an available subconnection to handle them.

Next add this snippet below TestPickerNoSubConnAvailable() to test pickers with subconnections to pick from:

ClientSideServiceDiscovery/internal/loadbalance/picker_test.go

```
func TestPickerProducesToLeader(t *testing.T) {
	picker, subConns := setupTest()
	info := balancer.PickInfo{
```

```
			FullMethodName: "/log.vX.Log/Produce",
		}
		for i := 0; i < 5; i++ {
			gotPick, err := picker.Pick(info)
			require.NoError(t, err)
			require.Equal(t, subConns[0], gotPick.SubConn)
		}
}

func TestPickerConsumesFromFollowers(t *testing.T) {
		picker, subConns := setupTest()
		info := balancer.PickInfo{
			FullMethodName: "/log.vX.Log/Consume",
		}
		for i := 0; i < 5; i++ {
			pick, err := picker.Pick(info)
			require.NoError(t, err)
			require.Equal(t, subConns[i%2+1], pick.SubConn)
		}
}
```

TestPickerProducesToLeader() tests that the picker picks the leader subconnection for append calls. TestPickerConsumesFromFollowers() tests that the picker picks the followers subconnections in a round-robin for consume calls.

Put this final snippet at the end of the file to define the tests' helpers:

ClientSideServiceDiscovery/internal/loadbalance/picker_test.go

```
func setupTest() (*loadbalance.Picker, []*subConn) {
	var subConns []*subConn
	buildInfo := base.PickerBuildInfo{
		ReadySCs: make(map[balancer.SubConn]base.SubConnInfo),
	}
	for i := 0; i < 3; i++ {
		sc := &subConn{}
		addr := resolver.Address{
			Attributes: attributes.New("is_leader", i == 0),
		}
		// 0th sub conn is the leader
		sc.UpdateAddresses([]resolver.Address{addr})
		buildInfo.ReadySCs[sc] = base.SubConnInfo{Address: addr}
		subConns = append(subConns, sc)
	}
	picker := &loadbalance.Picker{}
	picker.Build(buildInfo)
	return picker, subConns
}

// subConn implements balancer.SubConn.
type subConn struct {
	addrs []resolver.Address
}
```

```
func (s *subConn) UpdateAddresses(addrs []resolver.Address) {
	s.addrs = addrs
}

func (s *subConn) Connect() {}
```

setupTest() builds the test picker with some mock subconnections. We create the picker with build information that contains addresses with the same attributes as our resolver sets.

Run the picker's tests to verify they pass. Now we're ready to put everything together.

Test Discovery and Balancing End-to-End

We're ready to update our agent's tests to test everything end-to-end: the client configuring the resolver and picker, the resolver discovering the servers, and the picker picking subconnections per RPC.

Open your agent tests in internal/agent/agent_test.go and add this import:

ClientSideServiceDiscovery/internal/agent/agent_test.go

```
"github.com/travisjeffery/proglog/internal/loadbalance"
```

Then update the client() function to use your resolver and picker:

ClientSideServiceDiscovery/internal/agent/agent_test.go

```
func client(
	t *testing.T,
	agent *agent.Agent,
	tlsConfig *tls.Config,
) api.LogClient {
	tlsCreds := credentials.NewTLS(tlsConfig)
	opts := []grpc.DialOption{
		grpc.WithTransportCredentials(tlsCreds),
	}
	rpcAddr, err := agent.Config.RPCAddr()
	require.NoError(t, err)
	conn, err := grpc.Dial(fmt.Sprintf(
		"%s:///%s",
		loadbalance.Name,
		rpcAddr,
	), opts...)
	require.NoError(t, err)
	client := api.NewLogClient(conn)
	return client
}
```

The highlighted lines specify our scheme in the URL so gRPC knows to use our resolver.

Run the agent's tests by running `$ go run ./internal/agent`, and you'll see that the leader client consume call fails now. Why? Before, each client connected to one server. So the leader client connected to the leader. When we produced records, they were immediately available for consuming with the leader client because it consumed from the leader server—we didn't have to wait for the leader to replicate the record. Now, each client connects to every server and produces to the leader and consumes from the followers, so we must wait for the leader to replicate the record to the followers.

Update your test to wait for the servers to replicate the record before consuming with the leader client. Move `time.Sleep` that appears before line 14 to appear before line 4:

ClientSideServiceDiscovery/internal/agent/agent_test.go

```
1  // wait until replication has finished
2  time.Sleep(3 * time.Second)
3  
4  consumeResponse, err := leaderClient.Consume(
5  	context.Background(),
6  	&api.ConsumeRequest{
7  		Offset: produceResponse.Offset,
8  	},
9  )
10 require.NoError(t, err)
11 require.Equal(t, consumeResponse.Record.Value, []byte("foo"))
12 
13 followerClient := client(t, agents[1], peerTLSConfig)
14 consumeResponse, err = followerClient.Consume(
15 	context.Background(),
16 	&api.ConsumeRequest{
17 		Offset: produceResponse.Offset,
18 	},
19 )
20 require.NoError(t, err)
21 require.Equal(t, consumeResponse.Record.Value, []byte("foo"))
```

Run your tests again with `$ make test` and watch them pass!

What You Learned

Now you know how gRPC resolves services and balances calls across them and how you can build your own resolvers and pickers. You can write your own resolver so that your clients dynamically discover servers. And you saw how pickers are useful for more than just load balancing—you can build your own routing logic with them.

In the next part of the book, we'll look at how to deploy our service and make it live.

Part IV

Deploy

CHAPTER 10

Deploy Applications with Kubernetes Locally

After Frodo and Sam had trekked from the Shire to Mount Doom, was their task finished? No—the whole journey would've been for nothing if they hadn't thrown that ring into the fire. Likewise, building a service means something only after you've deployed it. Therefore, in this chapter, we'll deploy a cluster of our service. We'll:

- Create an agent command-line interface (CLI) so we have an executable to run our service.
- Get set up with Kubernetes and Helm so that we can orchestrate our service on both our local machine and later on a cloud platform.
- Run a cluster of your service on your machine.

Ready? Let's get started.

What Is Kubernetes?

While entire books are devoted to answering this question, even they can't cover everything Kubernetes can do. For our purposes in this book, I will touch upon the information you need to know to have a working knowledge of Kubernetes, enough to continue our journey and deploy and operate our service. Why Kubernetes? Kubernetes is ubiquitous, it's available on all cloud platforms, and it's as close to a standard as we have for deploying distributed services.

Kubernetes[1] is an open source orchestration system for automating deployment, scaling, and operating services running in containers. You tell Kubernetes what

1. https://kubernetes.io

to do by using its REST API to create, update, and delete resources that Kubernetes knows how to handle. Kubernetes is a declarative system in that you describe the end-goal state you want and Kubernetes runs the changes to take your system from its current state to your end-goal state.

The Kubernetes resource that people most commonly see are *pods*, the smallest deployable unit in Kubernetes. Think of containers as processes and pods as hosts—all containers running in a pod share the same network namespace, the same IP address, and the same interprocess communication (IPC) namespace, and they can share the same volumes. These are logical hosts because a physical host (what Kubernetes calls a *node*) may run multiple pods. The other resources you'll work with either configure pods (ConfigMaps, Secrets) or manage a pod set (Deployments, StatefulSets, DaemonSets). You can extend Kubernetes by creating your own custom resources and controllers.

Controllers are control loops that watch the state of your resources and make changes where needed. Kubernetes itself is made up of many controllers. For example, the Deployment controller watches your Deployment resources; if you increase the replicas on a Deployment, the controller will schedule more pods.

To interact with Kubernetes, you'll need its command-line tool, kubectl, which we'll look at next.

Install kubectl

The Kubernetes command-line tool, kubectl,[2] is used to run commands against Kubernetes clusters. You'll use kubectl to inspect and manage your service's cluster resources and view logs. Try to use kubectl for one-off operations. For operations you run again and again, like deploying or upgrading a service, you'll use the Helm package manager or an operator, which we'll take a look at later in this chapter.

To install kubectl, run the following:

```
$ curl -LO \
https://storage.googleapis.com/kubernetes-release/release/\
v1.18.0/bin/$(uname)/amd64/kubectl
$ chmod +x ./kubectl
$ mv ./kubectl /usr/local/bin/kubectl
```

We need a Kubernetes cluster and its API for kubectl to call and do anything. In the next section, we'll use the Kind tool to run a local Kubernetes cluster in Docker.

2. https://kubernetes.io/docs/reference/kubectl/overview

Use Kind for Local Development and Continuous Integration

Kind[3] (an acronym for *Kubernetes IN Docker*) is a tool developed by the Kubernetes team to run local Kubernetes clusters using Docker containers as nodes. It's the easiest way to run your own Kubernetes cluster, and it's great for local development, testing, and continuous integration.

To install Kind, run the following:

```
$ curl -Lo ./kind https://kind.sigs.k8s.io/dl/v0.8.1/kind-$(uname)-amd64
$ chmod +x ./kind
$ mv ./kind /usr/local/bin/kind
```

To use Kind, you'll need to install Docker.[4] See Docker's dedicated install instructions for your operation system.

With Docker running, you can create a Kind cluster by running:

```
$ kind create cluster
```

You can then verify that Kind created your cluster and configured kubectl to use it by running the following:

```
$ kubectl cluster-info
> Kubernetes master is running at https://127.0.0.1:46023
KubeDNS is running at \
https://127.0.0.1:46023/api/v1/namespaces/kube-system/services/kube-dns:dns/proxy
```

To further debug and diagnose cluster problems, use `kubectl cluster-info dump`.

Kind runs one Docker container representing one Kubernetes node in the cluster. By default, Kind runs a single node cluster with everything needed for a functioning Kubernetes cluster. You can see the Node container by running this:

```
$ docker ps
CONTAINER ID IMAGE COMMAND CREATED ...
033de99b1e53 kindest/node:v1.18.2 "/usr/local/bin/entr…" 2 minutes...
```

We have a running Kubernetes cluster now—let's run our service on it! To run our service in Kubernetes, we'll need a Docker image, and our Docker image will need an executable entry point. Let's write an agent CLI that serves as our service's executable.

3. https://kind.sigs.k8s.io
4. https://docs.docker.com/install

Write an Agent Command-Line Interface

Our agent CLI will provide just enough features to use as a Docker image's entry point and run our service, parse flags, and then configure and run the agent.

I use the Cobra[5] library to handle commands and flags because it works well for creating both simple CLIs and complex applications. It's used in the Go community by projects such as Kubernetes, Docker, Helm, Etcd, Hugo, and more. And Cobra integrates with a library called Viper,[6] which is a complete configuration solution for Go applications.

The first step is to create a cmd/proglog/main.go file, beginning with this code:

DeployLocally/cmd/proglog/main.go

```
package main

import (
	"log"
	"os"
	"os/signal"
	"path"
	"syscall"

	"github.com/spf13/cobra"
	"github.com/spf13/viper"
	"github.com/travisjeffery/proglog/internal/agent"
	"github.com/travisjeffery/proglog/internal/config"
)

func main() {
	cli := &cli{}

	cmd := &cobra.Command{
		Use:     "proglog",
		PreRunE: cli.setupConfig,
		RunE:    cli.run,
	}

	if err := setupFlags(cmd); err != nil {
		log.Fatal(err)
	}

	if err := cmd.Execute(); err != nil {
		log.Fatal(err)
	}
}
```

The highlighted code defines our sole command. Our CLI is about as simple as it gets. In more complex applications, this command would act as the root

5. https://github.com/spf13/cobra
6. https://github.com/spf13/viper

command tying together your subcommands. Cobra calls the RunE function you set on your command when the command runs. Put or call the command's primary logic in that function. Cobra enables you to run hook functions to run before and after RunE.

Cobra provides persistent flags and hooks for applications with many subcommands (so we're not using them in our program)—persistent flags and hooks apply to the current command and all its children. A common use case for a persistent flag is in API-wrapping CLIs. In these CLIs, every subcommand will need a flag for the API's endpoint address. In this situation, you'd use an --api-addr persistent flag that you declare once on the root command for all the subcommands to inherit.

To define our cli and cfg types, add the following code:

DeployLocally/cmd/proglog/main.go

```
type cli struct {
	cfg cfg
}

type cfg struct {
	agent.Config
	ServerTLSConfig config.TLSConfig
	PeerTLSConfig   config.TLSConfig
}
```

I typically create a cli struct in which I can put logic and data that's common to all the commands. I created a separate cfg struct from the agent.Config struct to handle the field types that we can't parse without error handling: the *net.TCPAddr and the *tls.Config.

Now, let's set up our CLI's flags.

Expose Flags

Below the previous snippet, add this code to declare our CLI's flags:

DeployLocally/cmd/proglog/main.go

```
func setupFlags(cmd *cobra.Command) error {
	hostname, err := os.Hostname()
	if err != nil {
		log.Fatal(err)
	}

	cmd.Flags().String("config-file", "", "Path to config file.")

	dataDir := path.Join(os.TempDir(), "proglog")
	cmd.Flags().String("data-dir",
		dataDir,
		"Directory to store log and Raft data.")
```

```
	cmd.Flags().String("node-name", hostname, "Unique server ID.")

	cmd.Flags().String("bind-addr",
		"127.0.0.1:8401",
		"Address to bind Serf on.")
	cmd.Flags().Int("rpc-port",
		8400,
		"Port for RPC clients (and Raft) connections.")
	cmd.Flags().StringSlice("start-join-addrs",
		nil,
		"Serf addresses to join.")
	cmd.Flags().Bool("bootstrap", false, "Bootstrap the cluster.")

	cmd.Flags().String("acl-model-file", "", "Path to ACL model.")
	cmd.Flags().String("acl-policy-file", "", "Path to ACL policy.")

	cmd.Flags().String("server-tls-cert-file", "", "Path to server tls cert.")
	cmd.Flags().String("server-tls-key-file", "", "Path to server tls key.")
	cmd.Flags().String("server-tls-ca-file",
		"",
		"Path to server certificate authority.")

	cmd.Flags().String("peer-tls-cert-file", "", "Path to peer tls cert.")
	cmd.Flags().String("peer-tls-key-file", "", "Path to peer tls key.")
	cmd.Flags().String("peer-tls-ca-file",
		"",
		"Path to peer certificate authority.")

	return viper.BindPFlags(cmd.Flags())
}
```

These flags allow people calling your CLI to configure the agent and learn the default configuration.

With the pflag.FlagSet.{{type}}Var() methods, we can set our configuration's values directly. However, the problem with setting the configurations directly is that not all types have supporting APIs out of the box. Our BindAddr configuration is an example, which is a *net.TCPAddr that we need to parse from a string. You can define custom flag values[7] when you have enough flags of the same type, or just use an intermediate value otherwise.

But what if we want to configure our service with more than flags, such as with a file? We'll look at how to read in the configuration from a file, too, for dynamic configurations.

Manage Your Configuration

Viper provides a centralized config registry system where multiple configuration sources can set the configuration but you can read the result in one place.

7. https://golang.org/pkg/flag/#Value

You could allow users to set the configuration with flags, a file, or by loading dynamic configs from a service like Consul—Viper supports all of these.

With a configuration file, you can support dynamic config changes to a running service. The service watches the config file for changes and updates accordingly. For example, you may run your service at INFO-level logs by default but need DEBUG-level logs when you're debugging an issue with the running service. A configuration file also enables other processes to set up the configuration for the service. We'll see an example of that with our service where we have an init container that sets up the configuration for the service's container.

I've given usable defaults for the configurations we have to set: the data directory, bind address, the RPC port, and the node name. Try to set usable default flag values instead of requiring users to set them.

After declaring the flags, the next step is to execute the root command to parse the process's arguments and search through the command tree to find the correct command to run. We just have the one command, so we're not making Cobra work hard.

Add this snippet to set up the config:

DeployLocally/cmd/proglog/main.go

```
func (c *cli) setupConfig(cmd *cobra.Command, args []string) error {
	var err error

	configFile, err := cmd.Flags().GetString("config-file")
	if err != nil {
		return err
	}
	viper.SetConfigFile(configFile)

	if err = viper.ReadInConfig(); err != nil {
		// it's ok if config file doesn't exist
		if _, ok := err.(viper.ConfigFileNotFoundError); !ok {
			return err
		}
	}

	c.cfg.DataDir = viper.GetString("data-dir")
	c.cfg.NodeName = viper.GetString("node-name")
	c.cfg.BindAddr = viper.GetString("bind-addr")
	c.cfg.RPCPort = viper.GetInt("rpc-port")
	c.cfg.StartJoinAddrs = viper.GetStringSlice("start-join-addrs")
	c.cfg.Bootstrap = viper.GetBool("bootstrap")
	c.cfg.ACLModelFile = viper.GetString("acl-mode-file")
	c.cfg.ACLPolicyFile = viper.GetString("acl-policy-file")
	c.cfg.ServerTLSConfig.CertFile = viper.GetString("server-tls-cert-file")
	c.cfg.ServerTLSConfig.KeyFile = viper.GetString("server-tls-key-file")
```

```
	c.cfg.ServerTLSConfig.CAFile = viper.GetString("server-tls-ca-file")
	c.cfg.PeerTLSConfig.CertFile = viper.GetString("peer-tls-cert-file")
	c.cfg.PeerTLSConfig.KeyFile = viper.GetString("peer-tls-key-file")
	c.cfg.PeerTLSConfig.CAFile = viper.GetString("peer-tls-ca-file")

	if c.cfg.ServerTLSConfig.CertFile != "" &&
		c.cfg.ServerTLSConfig.KeyFile != "" {
		c.cfg.ServerTLSConfig.Server = true
		c.cfg.Config.ServerTLSConfig, err = config.SetupTLSConfig(
			c.cfg.ServerTLSConfig,
		)
		if err != nil {
			return err
		}
	}

	if c.cfg.PeerTLSConfig.CertFile != "" &&
		c.cfg.PeerTLSConfig.KeyFile != "" {
		c.cfg.Config.PeerTLSConfig, err = config.SetupTLSConfig(
			c.cfg.PeerTLSConfig,
		)
		if err != nil {
			return err
		}
	}

	return nil
}
```

setupConfig(cmd *cobra.Command, args []string) reads the configuration and prepares the agent's configuration. Cobra calls setupConfig() before running the command's RunE function.

Finish writing the program by including this run() method:

DeployLocally/cmd/proglog/main.go

```
func (c *cli) run(cmd *cobra.Command, args []string) error {
	var err error
	agent, err := agent.New(c.cfg.Config)
	if err != nil {
		return err
	}
	sigc := make(chan os.Signal, 1)
	signal.Notify(sigc, syscall.SIGINT, syscall.SIGTERM)
	<-sigc
	return agent.Shutdown()
}
```

run(cmd *cobra.Command, args []string) runs our executable's logic by:

- Creating the agent;
- Handling signals from the operating system; and

- Shutting down the agent gracefully when the operating system terminates the program.

Okay, we have our executable that we can use as our Docker image's entry point, so let's write our Dockerfile and build the image.

Build Your Docker Image

Create a Dockerfile with this code:

DeployLocally/Dockerfile

```
FROM golang:1.14-alpine AS build
WORKDIR /go/src/proglog
COPY . .
RUN CGO_ENABLED=0 go build -o /go/bin/proglog ./cmd/proglog

FROM scratch
COPY --from=build /go/bin/proglog /bin/proglog
ENTRYPOINT ["/bin/proglog"]
```

Our Dockerfile uses multistage builds: one stage builds our service and one stage runs it. This makes our Dockerfile easy to read and maintain while keeping our build efficient and the image small.

The build stage uses the golang:1.14-alpine image because we need the Go compiler, our dependencies, and perhaps various system libraries. These take up disk space, and we don't need them after we have compiled our binary. In the second stage, we use the scratch empty image—the smallest Docker image. We copy our binary into this image, and this is the image we deploy.

You must statically compile your binaries for them to run in the scratch image because it doesn't contain the system libraries needed to run dynamically linked binaries. That's why we disable Cgo—the compiler links it dynamically. Using the scratch image helps with thinking of the containers as being immutable. Instead of exec'ing into a container and mutating the image by installing tools or changing the filesystem, you run a short-lived container that has the tool you need.

The next step is to add a target to your Makefile to build the Docker image by adding this snippet to the bottom of the file:

DeployLocally/Makefile

```
TAG ?= 0.0.1

build-docker:
	docker build -t github.com/travisjeffery/proglog:$(TAG) .
```

Then build the image and load it into your Kind cluster by running:

```
$ make build-docker
$ kind load docker-image github.com/travisjeffery/proglog:0.0.1
```

Now that we have our Docker image, let's look at how we can configure and run a cluster of our service in Kubernetes with Helm.

Configure and Deploy Your Service with Helm

Helm[8] is the package manager for Kubernetes that enables you to distribute and install services in Kubernetes. Helm packages are called *charts*. A chart defines all resources needed to run a service in a Kubernetes cluster—for example, its deployments, services, persistent volume claims, and so on. Charts on Kubernetes are like Debian packages on Debian or Homebrew formulas on macOS. As a service developer, you'll want to build and share a Helm chart for your service to make it easier for people to run your service. (And if you're dogfooding your own service, you'll get the same benefit.)

A *release* is a instance of running a chart. Each time you install a chart into Kubernetes, Helm creates a release. In the Debian package and Homebrew formula examples, releases are like processes.

And finally, *repositories* are where you share charts to and install charts from; they're like Debian sources and Homebrew taps.

To install Helm, run this command:

```
$ curl https://raw.githubusercontent.com/helm/helm/master/scripts/get-helm-3 \
    | bash
```

Before we write our own Helm chart, let's take Helm for a spin and install an existing chart. Bitnami[9] maintains a repository of charts for popular applications. Let's add a Bitnami repository and install the Nginx chart, which is a web and proxy server:

```
$ helm repo add bitnami https://charts.bitnami.com/bitnami
$ helm install my-nginx bitnami/nginx
```

We can see the releases by running `$ helm list`:

```
$ helm list
NAME            NAMESPACE       REVISION        UPDATED         STATUS...
my-nginx        default         1               2020...      deployed...
```

Let's request Nginx to confirm that it's really running:

8. https://helm.sh
9. https://bitnami.com/kubernetes

```
$ POD_NAME=$(kubectl get pod \
    --selector=app.kubernetes.io/name=nginx \
    --template '{{index .items 0 "metadata" "name" }}')
$ SERVICE_IP=$(kubectl get svc \
    --namespace default my-nginx --template "{{ .spec.clusterIP }}")
$ kubectl exec $POD_NAME curl $SERVICE_IP
  % Total    % Received % Xferd  Average Speed   Time    Time     Time  Current
                                 Dload  Upload   Total   Spent    Left  Speed
100   612  100   612    0     0   597k      0 --:--:-- --:--:-- --:--:--  597k
<!DOCTYPE html>
<html>
<head>
<title>Welcome to nginx!</title>
<style>
    body {
        width: 35em;
        margin: 0 auto;
        font-family: Tahoma, Verdana, Arial, sans-serif;
    }
</style>
</head>
<body>
<h1>Welcome to nginx!</h1>
<p>If you see this page, the nginx web server is successfully installed and
working. Further configuration is required.</p>

<p>For online documentation and support please refer to
<a href="http://nginx.org/">nginx.org</a>.<br/>
Commercial support is available at
<a href="http://nginx.com/">nginx.com</a>.</p>

<p><em>Thank you for using nginx.</em></p>
</body>
</html>
```

We could use the same technique for deploying Nginx in a production environment, aside from setting some configuration parameters to fit our use case. Helm made it easy to install and configure an Nginx cluster, and we can manage other services the same way.

Uninstall the Nginx release by running the following:

```
$ helm uninstall my-nginx
release "my-nginx" uninstalled
```

Now, let's build our own chart.

Build Your Own Helm Chart

In this section, we'll build a Helm chart for our service and use it to install a cluster in our Kind cluster.

Create your Helm chart by running these commands:

```
$ mkdir deploy && cd deploy
$ helm create proglog
```

Helm created a new chart in a new proglog directory that's bootstrapped with an example that shows you what a Helm chart looks like—to write your own or to tweak for your own services. The proglog directory contains these directories and files:

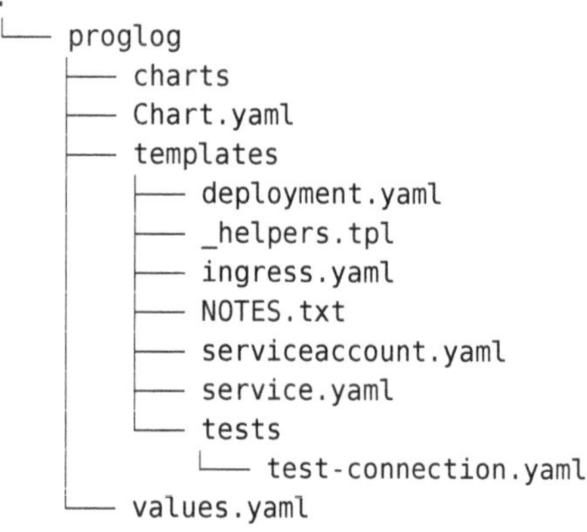

```
.
└── proglog
    ├── charts
    ├── Chart.yaml
    ├── templates
    │   ├── deployment.yaml
    │   ├── _helpers.tpl
    │   ├── ingress.yaml
    │   ├── NOTES.txt
    │   ├── serviceaccount.yaml
    │   ├── service.yaml
    │   └── tests
    │       └── test-connection.yaml
    └── values.yaml
```

```
4 directories, 9 files
```

The Chart.yaml file describes your chart. You can access the data in this file in your templates. The charts directory may contain subcharts, though I've never needed subcharts.

The values.yaml contains your chart's default values. Users can override these values when they install or upgrade your chart (for example, the port your service listens on, your service's resource requirements, log level, and so on).

The templates directory contains template files that you render with your values to generate valid Kubernetes manifest files. Kubernetes applies the rendered manifest files to install the resources needed for your service. You write your Helm templates using the Go template language.

You can render the templates locally without applying the resources in your Kubernetes cluster by running $ helm template. This is useful when you're developing your templates or if you want to apply your changes in a two-step plan-then-apply process because you can see the rendered resources that Kubernetes will apply.

To check out the resources Helm would create with the example chart, run this command:

```
$ helm template proglog
```

You'll see the following:

```
---
# Source: proglog/templates/serviceaccount.yaml
apiVersion: v1
kind: ServiceAccount
metadata:
  name: RELEASE-NAME-proglog
  labels:

    helm.sh/chart: proglog-0.1.0
    app.kubernetes.io/name: proglog
    app.kubernetes.io/instance: RELEASE-NAME
    app.kubernetes.io/version: "1.16.0"
    app.kubernetes.io/managed-by: Helm
---
# Source: proglog/templates/service.yaml
«rest»
```

We don't need the example templates, so remove them by running this command:

```
$ rm proglog/templates/**/*.yaml proglog/templates/NOTES.txt
```

Generally, Helm charts include a template file for each resource type. Our service will require two resource types: a StatefulSet and a Service, so we'll have a statefulset.yaml file and a service.yaml file. Let's begin with the StatefulSet.

StatefulSets in Kubernetes

You use StatefulSets to manage stateful applications in Kubernetes, like our service that persists a log. You need a StatefulSet for any service that requires one or more of the following:

- Stable, unique network identifiers—each node in our service requires unique node names as identifiers.
- Stable, persistent storage—our service expects the data its written to persist across restarts.
- Ordered, graceful deployment and scaling—our service needs initial node to bootstrap the cluster and join subsequent nodes to its cluster.
- Ordered, automated rolling updates—we always want our cluster to have a leader, and when we roll the leader we want to give the cluster enough time to elect a new leader before rolling the next node.

And by "stable," I mean persisted across scheduling changes like restarts and scaling.

If your service isn't stateful and doesn't require these features, then you should use a Deployment instead of a StatefulSet. One example is an API service that persists to a relational database, like Postgres. You'd run the API service with a Deployment because it's stateless, and you'd run Postgres with a StatefulSet.

Create a deploy/proglog/templates/statefulset.yaml file with this code:

DeployLocally/deploy/proglog/templates/statefulset.yaml
```
apiVersion: apps/v1
kind: StatefulSet
metadata:
  name: {{ include "proglog.fullname" . }}
  namespace: {{ .Release.Namespace }}
  labels: {{ include "proglog.labels" . | nindent 4 }}
spec:
  selector:
    matchLabels: {{ include "proglog.selectorLabels" . | nindent 6 }}
  serviceName: {{ include "proglog.fullname" . }}
  replicas: {{ .Values.replicas }}
  template:
    metadata:
      name: {{ include "proglog.fullname" . }}
      labels: {{ include "proglog.labels" . | nindent 8 }}
    spec:
      # initContainers...
      # containers...
  volumeClaimTemplates:
  - metadata:
      name: datadir
    spec:
      accessModes: [ "ReadWriteOnce" ]
      resources:
        requests:
          storage: {{ .Values.storage }}
```

I have omitted the spec's initContainers and containers fields to make the snippet smaller (we will fill those in next). The only thing of note here is that our StatefulSet has a datadir PersistentVolumeClaim—the claim requests storage for our cluster. Based on our configuration, Kubernetes could fulfill the claim with a local disk, a disk provided by your cloud platform, and so on. Kubernetes takes care of obtaining and binding the storage to your containers.

Now, replace initContainers... in the previous snippet with this code:

DeployLocally/deploy/proglog/templates/statefulset.yaml

```
initContainers:
- name: {{ include "proglog.fullname" . }}-config-init
  image: busybox
  imagePullPolicy: IfNotPresent
  command:
    - /bin/sh
    - -c
    - |-
      ID=$(echo $HOSTNAME | rev | cut -d- -f1 | rev)
      cat > /var/run/proglog/config.yaml <<EOD
      data-dir: /var/run/proglog/data
      rpc-port: {{.Values.rpcPort}}
      # Make sure the following three key-values are on one line each in
      # your code. I split them across multiple lines to fit them in
      # for the book.
      bind-addr: \
        "$HOSTNAME.proglog.{{.Release.Namespace}}.\svc.cluster.local:\
          {{.Values.serfPort}}"
      bootstrap: $([ $ID = 0 ] && echo true || echo false)
      $([ $ID != 0 ] && echo 'start-join-addrs: \
        "proglog-0.proglog.{{.Release.Namespace}}.svc.cluster.local:\
          {{.Values.serfPort}}"')
      EOD
  volumeMounts:
  - name: datadir
    mountPath: /var/run/proglog
```

Init containers run to completion before the StatefulSet's app containers listed in the containers field. Our config init container sets up our service's configuration file. We configure the first server to bootstrap the Raft cluster. And we configure the subsequent servers to join the cluster. We mount the datadir volume into the container so we can write to the same configuration file our app container will read from later.

Replace containers... in the previous snippet with this:

DeployLocally/deploy/proglog/templates/statefulset.yaml

```
containers:
- name: {{ include "proglog.fullname" . }}
  image: "{{ .Values.image.repository }}:{{ .Values.image.tag }}"
  ports:
  - containerPort: {{ .Values.rpcPort }}
    name: rpc
  - containerPort: {{ .Values.serfPort }}
    name: serf
  args:
    - --config-file=/var/run/proglog/config.yaml
```

```
# probes...
volumeMounts:
- name: datadir
  mountPath: /var/run/proglog
```

These containers define our StatefulSet's app containers; we need one for our service. We mount the volume to the container for reading the configuration file and persisting the log. We use a flag to tell our service where to find its configuration file.

Container Probes and gRPC Health Check

Kubernetes uses *probes* to know whether it needs to act on a container to improve your service's reliability. With a service, usually the probe requests a health check endpoint that responds with the health of the service.

There are three types of probes:

- *Liveness probes* signal that the container is alive, otherwise Kubernetes will restart the container. Kubernetes calls the liveness probe throughout the container's lifetime.
- *Readiness probes* check that the container is ready to accept traffic, otherwise Kubernetes will remove the pod from the service load balancers. Kubernetes calls the readiness probe throughout the container's lifetime.
- *Startup probes* signal when the container application has started and Kubernetes can begin probing for liveness and readiness. Distributed services often need to go through service discovery and join in consensus with the cluster before they're initialized. If we had a liveness probe that failed before our service finished initializing, our service would continually restart. After startup, Kubernetes doesn't call this probe again.

These probes should help improve your service's reliability, but they can cause incidents if they're not carefully implemented (like the example of the liveness probe that restarts the container before it's finished initializing). The systems dedicated to improving the reliability of the service can cause more incidents than the service by itself.

You have three ways of running probes:

- Making an HTTP request against a server;
- Opening a TCP socket against a server; and
- Running a command in the container (for example, Postgres has a command called `pg_isready` that connects to a Postgres server).

The first two are lightweight because they don't require any extra binaries in your image. However, a command can be more precise and necessary if you use your own protocol.

gRPC services conventionally use a grpc_health_probe command that expects your server to satisfy the gRPC health checking protocol.[10] Our server needs to export a service defined as:

```
syntax = "proto3";

package grpc.health.v1;

message HealthCheckRequest {
  string service = 1;
}

message HealthCheckResponse {
  enum ServingStatus {
    UNKNOWN = 0;
    SERVING = 1;
    NOT_SERVING = 2;
  }
  ServingStatus status = 1;
}

service Health {
  rpc Check(HealthCheckRequest) returns (HealthCheckResponse);

  rpc Watch(HealthCheckRequest) returns (stream HealthCheckResponse);
}
```

Let's update our server to export the health check service.

Open internal/server/server.go and add the highlighted imports:

DeployLocally/internal/server/server.go

```
import (
	"context"
	"time"

	api "github.com/travisjeffery/proglog/api/v1"

	grpc_middleware "github.com/grpc-ecosystem/go-grpc-middleware"
	grpc_auth "github.com/grpc-ecosystem/go-grpc-middleware/auth"
	grpc_zap "github.com/grpc-ecosystem/go-grpc-middleware/logging/zap"
	grpc_ctxtags "github.com/grpc-ecosystem/go-grpc-middleware/tags"

	"go.opencensus.io/plugin/ocgrpc"
	"go.opencensus.io/stats/view"
	"go.opencensus.io/trace"
```

10. https://github.com/grpc/grpc/blob/master/doc/health-checking.md

```
	"go.uber.org/zap"
	"go.uber.org/zap/zapcore"

	"google.golang.org/grpc"
	"google.golang.org/grpc/codes"
	"google.golang.org/grpc/credentials"
	"google.golang.org/grpc/peer"
	"google.golang.org/grpc/status"

➤	"google.golang.org/grpc/health"
➤	healthpb "google.golang.org/grpc/health/grpc_health_v1"
)
```

Then, update the NewGRPCServer() function to include the highlighted lines in this snippet:

DeployLocally/internal/server/server.go

```
func NewGRPCServer(config *Config, grpcOpts ...grpc.ServerOption) (
	*grpc.Server,
	error,
) {
	logger := zap.L().Named("server")
	zapOpts := []grpc_zap.Option{
		grpc_zap.WithDurationField(
			func(duration time.Duration) zapcore.Field {
				return zap.Int64(
					"grpc.time_ns",
					duration.Nanoseconds(),
				)
			},
		),
	}

	trace.ApplyConfig(trace.Config{
		DefaultSampler: trace.AlwaysSample(),
	})
	err := view.Register(ocgrpc.DefaultServerViews...)
	if err != nil {
		return nil, err
	}

	grpcOpts = append(grpcOpts,
		grpc.StreamInterceptor(
			grpc_middleware.ChainStreamServer(
				grpc_ctxtags.StreamServerInterceptor(),
				grpc_zap.StreamServerInterceptor(
					logger, zapOpts...,
				),
				grpc_auth.StreamServerInterceptor(
					authenticate,
				),
			)), grpc.UnaryInterceptor(
			grpc_middleware.ChainUnaryServer(
```

```
                                grpc_ctxtags.UnaryServerInterceptor(),
                                grpc_zap.UnaryServerInterceptor(
                                        logger, zapOpts...,
                                ),
                                grpc_auth.UnaryServerInterceptor(
                                        authenticate,
                                ),
                        )),
                grpc.StatsHandler(&ocgrpc.ServerHandler{}),
        )
        gsrv := grpc.NewServer(grpcOpts...)
➤       hsrv := health.NewServer()
➤       hsrv.SetServingStatus("", healthpb.HealthCheckResponse_SERVING)
➤       healthpb.RegisterHealthServer(gsrv, hsrv)
        srv, err := newgrpcServer(config)
        if err != nil {
                return nil, err
        }
        api.RegisterLogServer(gsrv, srv)
        return gsrv, nil
}
```

These lines create a service that supports the health check protocol. We set its serving status as serving so that the probe knows the service is alive and ready to accept connections. Then we register the service with our server so that gRPC can call this service's endpoints.

Replace probes... in deploy/proglog/templates/statefulset.yaml with this snippet to tell Kubernetes how to probe our service:

DeployLocally/deploy/proglog/templates/statefulset.yaml

```
readinessProbe:
  exec:
    command: ["/bin/grpc_health_probe", "-addr=:{{ .Values.rpcPort }}"]
  initialDelaySeconds: 10
livenessProbe:
  exec:
    command: ["/bin/grpc_health_probe", "-addr=:{{ .Values.rpcPort }}"]
  initialDelaySeconds: 10
```

Then add these highlighted lines to your Dockerfile to install the grpc_health_probe executable in your image:

DeployLocally/Dockerfile

```
FROM golang:1.14-alpine AS build
WORKDIR /go/src/proglog
COPY . .
RUN CGO_ENABLED=0 go build -o /go/bin/proglog ./cmd/proglog
➤ RUN GRPC_HEALTH_PROBE_VERSION=v0.3.2 && \
```

```
    wget -qO/go/bin/grpc_health_probe \
    https://github.com/grpc-ecosystem/grpc-health-probe/releases/download/\
    ${GRPC_HEALTH_PROBE_VERSION}/grpc_health_probe-linux-amd64 && \
    chmod +x /go/bin/grpc_health_probe

FROM scratch
COPY --from=build /go/bin/proglog /bin/proglog
COPY --from=build /go/bin/grpc_health_probe /bin/grpc_health_probe
ENTRYPOINT ["/bin/proglog"]
```

The last resource we need to define in our Helm chart is the Service.

Kubernetes Services

A *Service* in Kubernetes exposes an application as a network service. You define a Service with policies that specify what Pods the Service applies to and how to access the Pods.

Four types of services specify how the Service exposes the Pods:

- *ClusterIP* exposes the Service on a load-balanced cluster-internal IP so the Service is reachable within the Kubernetes cluster only. This is the default Service type.
- *NodePort* exposes the Service on each Node's IP on a static port—even if the Node doesn't have a Pod on it, Kubernetes sets up the routing so if you request a Node at the service's port, it'll direct the request to the proper place. You can request NodePort services outside the Kubernetes cluster.
- *LoadBalancer* exposes the Service externally using a cloud provider's load balancer. A LoadBalancer Service automatically creates ClusterIP and NodeIP services behind the scenes and manages the routes to these services.
- *ExternalName* is a special Service that serves as a way to alias a DNS name.

I don't recommend using NodePort services (aside from the ones LoadBalancer services create for you). You have to know your nodes' IPs to use the services, you must secure all your Nodes, and you have to deal with port conflicts. Instead, I recommend using a LoadBalancer or a ClusterIP service if you're able to run a Pod that can access your internal network.

Create a deploy/proglog/templates/service.yaml for your service template with the following code:

DeployLocally/deploy/proglog/templates/service.yaml

```
apiVersion: v1
kind: Service
metadata:
  name: {{ include "proglog.fullname" . }}
  namespace: {{ .Release.Namespace }}
  labels: {{ include "proglog.labels" . | nindent 4 }}
spec:
  clusterIP: None
  publishNotReadyAddresses: true
  ports:
    - name: rpc
      port: {{ .Values.rpcPort }}
      targetPort: {{ .Values.rpcPort }}
    - name: serf-tcp
      protocol: "TCP"
      port: {{ .Values.serfPort }}
      targetPort: {{ .Values.serfPort }}
    - name: serf-udp
      protocol: "UDP"
      port: {{ .Values.serfPort }}
      targetPort: {{ .Values.serfPort }}
  selector: {{ include "proglog.selectorLabels" . | nindent 4 }}
```

This snippet defines our "headless" Service. A headless Service doesn't load balance to a single IP. You use a headless Service when your distributed service has its own means for service discovery. By defining selectors on our Service, Kubernetes' endpoint controller changes the DNS configuration to return records that point to the Pods backing the Service. So, each pod will get its own DNS record similar to proglog-{{id}}.proglog.{{namespace}}.svc.cluster.local, and the servers will use these records to discover each other.

Advertise Raft on the Fully Qualified Domain Name

Currently, we configure Raft's address as the transport's local address, and the server will advertise its address as ::8400. We want to use the fully qualified domain name instead so the node will properly advertise itself to its cluster and to its clients.

In internal/log/config.go, change your Config to this:

DeployLocally/internal/log/config.go

```
type Config struct {
	Raft struct {
		raft.Config
		BindAddr string
		StreamLayer *StreamLayer
		Bootstrap   bool
	}
```

```
        Segment struct {
                MaxStoreBytes uint64
                MaxIndexBytes uint64
                InitialOffset uint64
        }
}
```

Change your DistributedLog's bootstrap code to use the configured bind address:

DeployLocally/internal/log/distributed.go

```
if l.config.Raft.Bootstrap && !hasState {
        config := raft.Configuration{
                Servers: []raft.Server{{
                        ID:      config.LocalID,
                        Address: raft.ServerAddress(l.config.Raft.BindAddr),
                }},
        }
        err = l.raft.BootstrapCluster(config).Error()
}
```

And in distributed_test.go, update your log configuration to set the address:

DeployLocally/internal/log/distributed_test.go

```
config := log.Config{}
config.Raft.StreamLayer = log.NewStreamLayer(ln, nil, nil)
config.Raft.LocalID = raft.ServerID(fmt.Sprintf("%d", i))
config.Raft.HeartbeatTimeout = 50 * time.Millisecond
config.Raft.ElectionTimeout = 50 * time.Millisecond
config.Raft.LeaderLeaseTimeout = 50 * time.Millisecond
config.Raft.CommitTimeout = 5 * time.Millisecond
config.Raft.BindAddr = ln.Addr().String()
```

Run your log tests to verify they pass.

Finally, in agent.go, update setupMux() and setupLog() to configure the mux and Raft instance:

DeployLocally/internal/agent/agent.go

```
func (a *Agent) setupMux() error {
        addr, err := net.ResolveTCPAddr("tcp", a.Config.BindAddr)
        if err != nil {
                return err
        }
        rpcAddr := fmt.Sprintf(
                "%s:%d",
                addr.IP.String(),
                a.Config.RPCPort,
        )
        ln, err := net.Listen("tcp", rpcAddr)
        if err != nil {
                return err
        }
```

```
        a.mux = cmux.New(ln)
        return nil
}

func (a *Agent) setupLog() error {
        // ...
        logConfig := log.Config{}
        logConfig.Raft.StreamLayer = log.NewStreamLayer(
                raftLn,
                a.Config.ServerTLSConfig,
                a.Config.PeerTLSConfig,
        )
➤       rpcAddr, err := a.Config.RPCAddr()
➤       if err != nil {
➤               return err
➤       }
➤       logConfig.Raft.BindAddr = rpcAddr
        logConfig.Raft.LocalID = raft.ServerID(a.Config.NodeName)
        logConfig.Raft.Bootstrap = a.Config.Bootstrap
        // ...
}
```

Now we're ready to deploy the service in our Kubernetes cluster.

Install Your Helm Chart

We've finished writing our Helm chart and we can install it in our Kind cluster to run a cluster of our service.

You can see what Helm renders by running:

```
$ helm template proglog deploy/proglog
```

You'll see that the repository is still set to the default: nginx. Open up deploy/proglog/values.yaml and replace the entire contents to look like this:

DeployLocally/deploy/proglog/values.yaml

```
# Default values for proglog.
image:
  repository: github.com/travisjeffery/proglog
  tag: 0.0.1
  pullPolicy: IfNotPresent
serfPort: 8401
rpcPort: 8400
replicas: 3
storage: 1Gi
```

The point of the values.yml is to set good defaults and show what parameters users can set if they must.

Now, install the Chart by running this command:

```
$ helm install proglog deploy/proglog
```

Wait a few seconds and you'll see Kubernetes set up three pods. You can list them by running `$ kubectl get pods`. When all three pods are ready, we can try requesting the API.

We can tell Kubernetes to forward a pod or a Service's port to a port on your computer so you can request a service running inside Kubernetes without a load balancer:

```
$ kubectl port-forward pod/proglog-0 8400 8400
```

Now we can request our service from a program running outside Kubernetes at `:8400`.

Let's write a simple executable to get the list of servers. Create a file named `cmd/getservers/main.go` that looks like this:

DeployLocally/cmd/getservers/main.go

```
package main

import (
	"context"
	"flag"
	"fmt"
	"log"

	api "github.com/travisjeffery/proglog/api/v1"
	"google.golang.org/grpc"
)

func main() {
	addr := flag.String("addr", ":8400", "service address")
	flag.Parse()
	conn, err := grpc.Dial(*addr, grpc.WithInsecure())
	if err != nil {
		log.Fatal(err)
	}
	client := api.NewLogClient(conn)
	ctx := context.Background()
	res, err := client.GetServers(ctx, &api.GetServersRequest{})
	if err != nil {
		log.Fatal(err)
	}
	fmt.Println("servers:")
	for _, server := range res.Servers {
		fmt.Printf("\t- %v\n", server)
	}
}
```

Then, run the command to request our service to get and print the list of servers:

```
$ go run cmd/getservers/main.go
```

You should see the following output:

```
servers:
- id:"proglog-0" rpc_addr:"proglog-0.proglog.default.svc.cluster.local:8400"
- id:"proglog-1" rpc_addr:"proglog-1.proglog.default.svc.cluster.local:8400"
- id:"proglog-2" rpc_addr:"proglog-2.proglog.default.svc.cluster.local:8400"
```

This means all three servers in our cluster have successfully joined the cluster and are coordinating with each other!

What You Learned

In this chapter, you learned the fundamentals of Kubernetes and how to use Kind to set up a Kubernetes cluster that you can run on your machine or on a CI. You also learned how to create a Helm chart and how to install your Helm chart into Kubernetes to run a cluster of your service. You learned quite a lot! In the next chapter, we'll build on this knowledge and deploy your service on a cloud platform.

CHAPTER 11

Deploy Applications with Kubernetes to the Cloud

In the previous chapter, we put the work into making our service deployable, but we only deployed it locally. In this chapter, we'll deploy our service to the cloud and put it on the Internet. Kubernetes abstracts the resources needed for your applications—containers, networking, volumes, and so on—similar to how Go abstracts the operating system and processor architecture so you can run the same program on each. As such, the changes you need to make to take your local Kubernetes cluster to the cloud can be little to nothing.

Three major cloud platforms dominate the landscape: Google Cloud Platform (GCP),[1] Amazon Web Services (AWS),[2] and Microsoft Azure.[3] All three platforms provide similar feature sets and their own Kubernetes services. With Kubernetes making up the differences between the platforms, we can deploy to any one, easily move between providers (and bargain with the providers for better prices), or run across them all at the same time. In this chapter, we'll deploy our service to the Google Cloud Platform.

GCP provides a free tier of products, with limitations, along with $300 credit to spend during your twelve-month free trial. What matters to us for purposes of our work in this book is that the free tier includes one Kubernetes cluster and 5 GB of storage—good enough to deploy our service to the cloud. Though Google won't charge you for the free trial, you need a credit card to sign up, and during the trial, Google displays a banner showing how many credits and how much time you have left so you know your status. Once your trial

1. https://cloud.google.com
2. https://aws.amazon.com
3. https://azure.microsoft.com/en-us

is over and/or you decide to purchase the service and use more of the platform, Google requires you to enable automatic billing.

Create a Google Kubernetes Engine Cluster

Let's start by getting you set up with Google Cloud by creating an account and Google Kubernetes Engine (GKE) cluster and configuring your computer's Docker and kubectl to work with the cloud services. GKE is GCP's managed Kubernetes service, enabling you to create a Kubernetes cluster with a single-click. GKE clusters are managed by Google's Site Reliability Engineers, who ensure that your cluster is available and up-to-date so that you can focus on your applications instead of Kubernetes.

Sign Up with Google Cloud

Open the GCP sign-up form[4] and log in to your existing Google account or make a new account. Follow the form instructions, filling in the form with your details until you've started your free trial. Then continue to the next step to create a Kubernetes cluster.

Create a Kubernetes Cluster

Navigate to the Kubernetes Engine service[5] and click Create cluster to open the cluster creation form shown in the screenshot that follows. In the form, change the name field from its default cluster-1 to proglog. Keep the location type as its default (Zonal). In the master version section, select the Release channel radio and select the current Regular channel, which is 1.16.11-gke.5 as I write this. Then click the Create button at the bottom of the page. The page will refresh and show a spinner that indicates GCP is provisioning the cluster. You'll see a green check mark when the cluster is ready, as shown on page 221.

Install and Authenticate gcloud

Google Cloud provides a cloud software development kit (SDK) with various tools and libraries for working with Google's services. The SDK includes the gcloud CLI, which we need to interact with the Google Cloud APIs and configure Docker. Install the latest Cloud SDK by following the installation instructions for your OS from the Google Cloud Developer Tools page.[6]

---

4. https://console.cloud.google.com/freetrial/signup/tos?pli=1
5. https://console.cloud.google.com/kubernetes
6. https://cloud.google.com/sdk/docs/downloads-versioned-archives

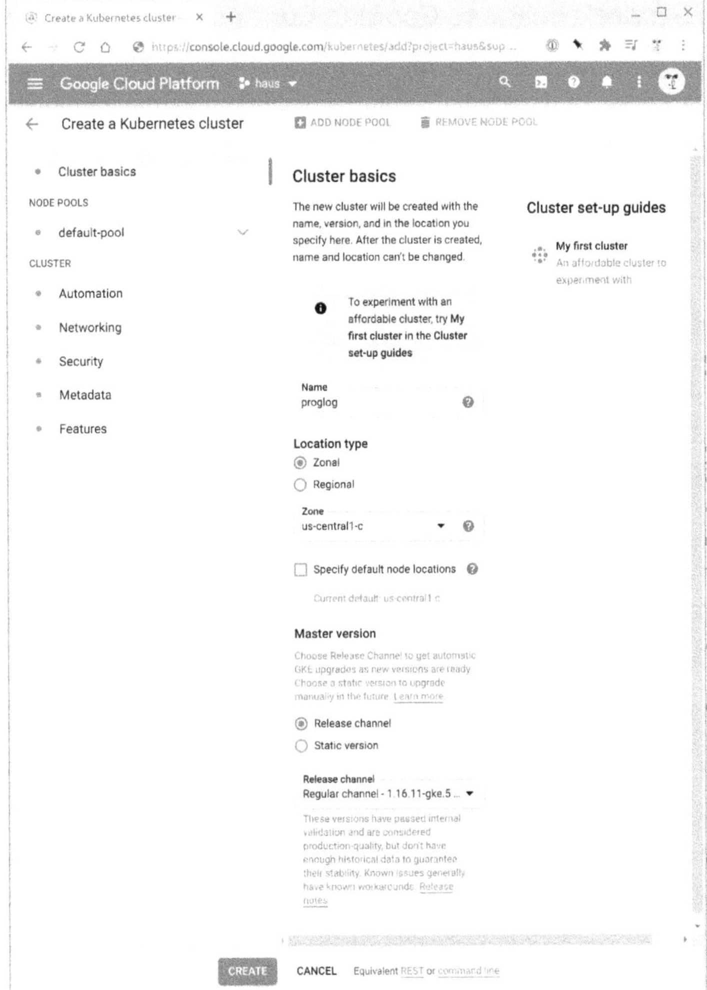

After you've installed the gcloud CLI, authenticate the CLI for your account by running this command:

```
$ gcloud auth login
```

Now that you've authenticated the CLI, you can run gcloud commands against resources in your account. Get your project's ID, and configure gcloud to use the project by default by running the following:

```
$ PROJECT_ID=$(gcloud projects list | tail -n 1 | cut -d' ' -f1)
$ gcloud config set project $PROJECT_ID
```

We'll refer this PROJECT_ID environment variable several times, so if you make a new terminal session, make sure you set the variable again.

Push Our Service's Image to Google's Container Registry

We need to make our service's image pullable by our GKE cluster's nodes by pushing its image to Google's Container Registry. Run the following to push the image to the registry:

```
$ gcloud auth configure-docker
$ docker tag github.com/travisjeffery/proglog:0.0.1 \
    gcr.io/$PROJECT_ID/proglog:0.0.1
$ docker push gcr.io/$PROJECT_ID/proglog:0.0.1
```

The first line configures Docker to use Google's Container Registry and use gcloud as the credential helper for those registries. You can open your Docker configuration file (at ~/.docker/config.json by default) to see the configuration changes. The second line creates a new tag for the gcr.io registry name. The gcr.io registry hosts images in the United States (though that may change). You'll also find us.gcr.io, eu.gcr.io, and asia.gcr.io if you need your images in specific regions. The third line pushes the image to the registry.

Configure kubectl

The last bit of setup allows kubectl and Helm to call our GKE cluster:

```
$ gcloud container clusters get-credentials proglog --zone us-central1-c
Fetching cluster endpoint and auth data.
kubeconfig entry generated for proglog.
```

This command updates your kubeconfig file (at ~/.kube/config by default) with the credentials and configuration to point kubectl at your cluster in GKE. Helm uses the kubeconfig file, too.

Okay, we've set up our Google Cloud project, created a GKE cluster, and configured our clients to manage the cluster. We could deploy our service as-is to GKE, but Kubernetes won't make our service available on the Internet with our current deployment setup.

Let's fix that.

Create Custom Controllers with Metacontroller

We could deploy our service with no changes and our service would function the same as it did in our local Kind cluster. But we want to extend our deployment setup to expose our service on the Internet. Because our service load balances client-side, each pod needs its own static IP, so we need a load balancer service for each pod. It'd be nice for Kubernetes to automatically create the load balancers as the pods scale up and delete them as the pods scale down, but Kubernetes doesn't support this out of the box.

Enter Metacontroller.

Metacontroller[7] is a Kubernetes add-on that makes it easy to write and deploy custom controllers with simple scripts. Metacontroller lets us hook into Kubernetes' changes so that we can compose with our own changes. Metacontroller handles all the interactions with Kubernetes' API, including running a level-triggered reconciliation loop on your behalf. You just receive JSON describing Kubernetes' observed state and return JSON describing your desired state. You can build features in Kubernetes that would require writing an Operator[8] (a popular pattern for extending Kubernetes), with less code and effort than an Operator requires.

Install Metacontroller

To install Metacontroller, we need to apply a couple YAML files that define Metacontroller's APIs and RBAC authorization that enable the APIs to manage the Kubernetes cluster's resources. You can use two Metacontroller APIs:

- CompositeController, which is used to manage child resources based on some parent resource. The Deployment and StatefulSet controllers fit this pattern.
- DecoratorController, which is used to add behavior to a resource. This is the controller pattern we need and will build for our service-per-pod feature.

Next, we use Helm to install Metacontroller. From the root of your project, run the following commands to define the Metacontroller Helm chart:

```
$ cd deploy
$ helm create metacontroller
$ rm metacontroller/templates/**/*.yaml \
    metacontroller/templates/NOTES.txt \
    metacontroller/values.yaml
$ MC_URL=https://raw.githubusercontent.com\
/GoogleCloudPlatform/metacontroller/master/manifests/
$ curl -L $MC_URL/metacontroller-rbac.yaml > \
    metacontroller/templates/metacontroller-rbac.yaml
$ curl -L $MC_URL/metacontroller.yaml > \
    metacontroller/templates/metacontroller.yaml
```

Then install the Metacontroller chart by running these:

```
$ kubectl create namespace metacontroller
$ helm install metacontroller metacontroller
```

7. https://metacontroller.app
8. https://coreos.com/blog/introducing-operators.html

Now we can update our proglog chart to support our service-per-pod feature and then deploy our service to the cloud.

Add Service-per-Pod Load Balancer Hooks

We'll create a DecoratorController that adds a load balancer service for each pod in our service's StatefulSet.

Create a deploy/proglog/templates/service-per-pod.yaml file with the following code to define our DecoratorController and Metacontroller configuration:

DeployToCloud/deploy/proglog/templates/service-per-pod.yaml

```
{{ if .Values.service.lb }}
apiVersion: metacontroller.k8s.io/v1alpha1
kind: DecoratorController
metadata:
  name: service-per-pod
spec:
  resources:
  - apiVersion: apps/v1
    resource: statefulsets
    annotationSelector:
      matchExpressions:
      - {key: service-per-pod-label, operator: Exists}
      - {key: service-per-pod-ports, operator: Exists}
  attachments:
  - apiVersion: v1
    resource: services
  hooks:
    sync:
      webhook:
        url: "http://service-per-pod.metacontroller/create-service-per-pod"
    finalize:
      webhook:
        url: "http://service-per-pod.metacontroller/delete-service-per-pod"
```

Our DecoratorController decorates every StatefulSet with the service-per-pod-label and service-per-pod-ports annotations. The hooks field defines which hooks the controller will call. The sync hook should create and maintain the resources you desire for your StatefulSet. The finalize adds a finalizer to the StatefulSet that prevents Kubernetes from deleting the StatefulSet until the hook has had its chance to run and clean up its resources. Currently Metacontroller supports running webhooks, so we need an internal service and deployment to run the webhooks.

Put this snippet after the previous snippet to define the webhook service and its configuration:

DeployToCloud/deploy/proglog/templates/service-per-pod.yaml

```
---
apiVersion: v1
kind: ConfigMap
metadata:
  namespace: metacontroller
  name: service-per-pod-hooks
data:
{{ (.Files.Glob "hooks/*").AsConfig | indent 2 }}
---
apiVersion: apps/v1
kind: Deployment
metadata:
  name: service-per-pod
  namespace: metacontroller
spec:
  replicas: 1
  selector:
    matchLabels:
      app: service-per-pod
  template:
    metadata:
      labels:
        app: service-per-pod
    spec:
      containers:
      - name: hooks
        image: metacontroller/jsonnetd:0.1
        imagePullPolicy: Always
        workingDir: /hooks
        volumeMounts:
        - name: hooks
          mountPath: /hooks
      volumes:
      - name: hooks
        configMap:
          name: service-per-pod-hooks
---
apiVersion: v1
kind: Service
metadata:
  name: service-per-pod
  namespace: metacontroller
spec:
  selector:
    app: service-per-pod
  ports:
  - port: 80
    targetPort: 8080
{{ end }}
```

This code snippet defines our webhook, Deployment and Service, with a ConfigMap that mounts our hook code files. Our controller calls the http://service-per-pod.metacontroller/create-service-per-pod endpoint when the StatefulSet changes, and calls the http://service-per-pod.metacontroller/delete-service-per-pod endpoint when the StatefulSet is deleted. The paths of the endpoints match the names of our hook filenames.

Create a hooks directory to put the hook code in:

```
$ mkdir deploy/proglog/hooks
```

Add the hook to create the services by adding this create-service-per-pod.jsonnet file in the hooks directory:

DeployToCloud/deploy/proglog/hooks/create-service-per-pod.jsonnet

```
function(request) {
  local statefulset = request.object,
  local labelKey = statefulset.metadata.annotations["service-per-pod-label"],
  local ports = statefulset.metadata.annotations["service-per-pod-ports"],

  attachments: [
    {
      apiVersion: "v1",
      kind: "Service",
      metadata: {
        name: statefulset.metadata.name + "-" + index,
        labels: {app: "service-per-pod"}
      },
      spec: {
        type: "LoadBalancer",
        selector: {
          [labelKey]: statefulset.metadata.name + "-" + index
        },
        ports: [
          {
            local parts = std.split(portnums, ":"),
            port: std.parseInt(parts[0]),
            targetPort: std.parseInt(parts[1]),
          }
          for portnums in std.split(ports, ",")
        ]
      }
    }
    for index in std.range(0, statefulset.spec.replicas - 1)
  ]
}
```

We've implemented our hook in Jsonnet,[9] a data templating language that simply extends JSON with variables, conditionals, arithmetic, functions, imports, and errors. Kubernetes passes the StatefulSet we've decorated into the function. Our implementation iterates over each replica in the StatefulSet and builds a list of service attachments. We can attach arbitrary resources that are only connected to the target resource through owner references, meaning Kubernetes will delete them if the StatefulSet is deleted.

Next, add the hook to delete the service:

DeployToCloud/deploy/proglog/hooks/delete-service-per-pod.jsonnet

```
function(request) {
  attachments: [],
  finalized: std.length(request.attachments['Service.v1']) == 0
}
```

If the StatefulSet doesn't match our decorator selector or the StatefulSet is deleted, then we delete any attachments we've made. If we observe that all the services are gone, we mark the StatefulSet as finalized so Kubernetes can delete it.

Last, we must update our StatefulSet and set the annotations that signal Kubernetes to decorate this StatefulSet and create a service for each pod. Change the StatefulSet's metadata defined in statefulset.yaml to include these annotations:

DeployToCloud/deploy/proglog/templates/statefulset.yaml

```
apiVersion: apps/v1
kind: StatefulSet
metadata:
  name: {{ include "proglog.fullname" . }}
  namespace: {{ .Release.Namespace }}
  labels: {{ include "proglog.labels" . | nindent 4 }}
  {{ if .Values.service.lb }}
  annotations:
    service-per-pod-label: "statefulset.kubernetes.io/pod-name"
    service-per-pod-ports: "{{.Values.rpcPort}}:{{.Values.rpcPort}}"
  {{ end }}
spec:
  # ...
```

And that's all of our Metacontroller changes. Our service should create a load balancer service for each pod now. Let's deploy our service to our GKE cluster and try it!

9. https://jsonnet.org

Deploy to the Internet

This is the moment we've been building up to over the course of the book: deploying our distributed service to the cloud. Run the following command:

```
$ helm install proglog proglog \
    --set image.repository=gcr.io/$PROJECT_ID/proglog \
    --set service.lb=true
```

This command installs our proglog chart to our GKE cluster. We've set the image repository to configure the StatefulSet to pull the image from the Google Container Registry. And we've enabled the service-per-pod controller. You can watch as the services come up by passing the `-w` flag:

```
$ kubectl get services -w
```

When all three load balancers are up, we can verify that our client connects to our service running in the cloud and that our service nodes discovered each other:

```
$ ADDR=$(kubectl get service \
    -l app=service-per-pod \
    -o go-template=\
    '{{range .items}}\
        {{(index .status.loadBalancer.ingress 0).ip}}{{"\n"}}\
    {{end}}'\
    | head -n 1)
$ go run cmd/getservers/main.go -addr=$ADDR:8400
servers:
- id:"proglog-0" rpc_addr:"proglog-0.proglog.default.svc.cluster.local:8400"
- id:"proglog-1" rpc_addr:"proglog-1.proglog.default.svc.cluster.local:8400"
- id:"proglog-2" rpc_addr:"proglog-2.proglog.default.svc.cluster.local:8400"
```

What You Learned

Congratulations! You deployed your service to the cloud. Now any person on the Internet can use your service. You set up a Google Cloud account, a project, and a GKE cluster. You also learned how to write a simple controller to extend the behavior of Kubernetes resources with Metacontroller.

We've now reached the end of the book, and you've accomplished a lot. You've made a distributed service from scratch. You've learned distributed computing ideas like service discovery, consensus, and load balancing. You're ready to make your own distributed services and contribute to existing projects.[10]

Go leave your mark on this growing field!

---

10. https://github.com/avelino/awesome-go#distributed-systems

Index

Thank you!

How did you enjoy this book? Please let us know. Take a moment and email us at support@pragprog.com with your feedback. Tell us your story and you could win free ebooks. Please use the subject line "Book Feedback."

Ready for your next great Pragmatic Bookshelf book? Come on over to https://pragprog.com and use the coupon code BUYANOTHER2021 to save 30% on your next ebook.

Void where prohibited, restricted, or otherwise unwelcome. Do not use ebooks near water. If rash persists, see a doctor. Doesn't apply to *The Pragmatic Programmer* ebook because it's older than the Pragmatic Bookshelf itself. Side effects may include increased knowledge and skill, increased marketability, and deep satisfaction. Increase dosage regularly.

And thank you for your continued support,

Andy Hunt, Publisher

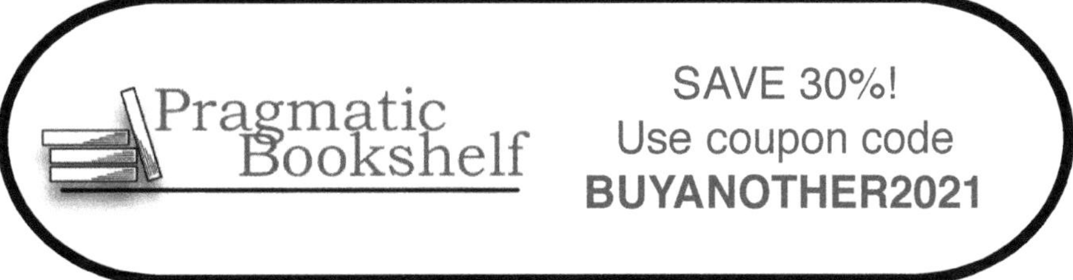

Explore Software Defined Radio

Do you want to be able to receive satellite images using nothing but your computer, an old TV antenna, and a $20 USB stick? Now you can. At last, the technology exists to turn your computer into a super radio receiver, capable of tuning in to FM, shortwave, amateur "ham," and even satellite frequencies, around the world and above it. Listen to police, fire, and aircraft signals, both in the clear and encoded. And with the book's advanced antenna design, there's no limit to the signals you can receive.

Wolfram Donat
(78 pages) ISBN: 9781680507591. $19.95
https://pragprog.com/book/wdradio

Genetic Algorithms in Elixir

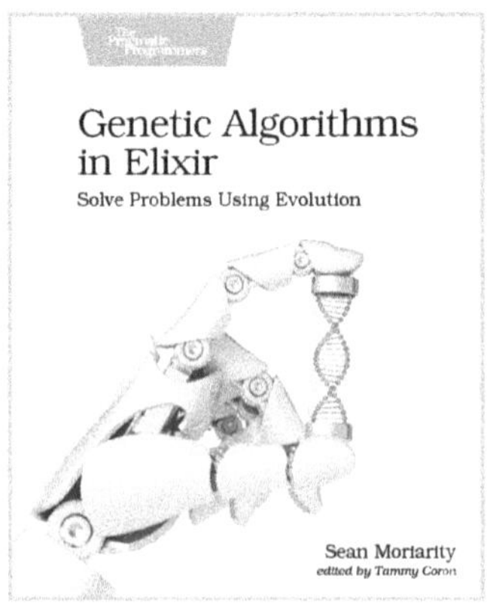

From finance to artificial intelligence, genetic algorithms are a powerful tool with a wide array of applications. But you don't need an exotic new language or framework to get started; you can learn about genetic algorithms in a language you're already familiar with. Join us for an in-depth look at the algorithms, techniques, and methods that go into writing a genetic algorithm. From introductory problems to real-world applications, you'll learn the underlying principles of problem solving using genetic algorithms.

Sean Moriarity
(242 pages) ISBN: 9781680507942. $39.95
https://pragprog.com/book/smgaelixir

Design and Build Great Web APIs

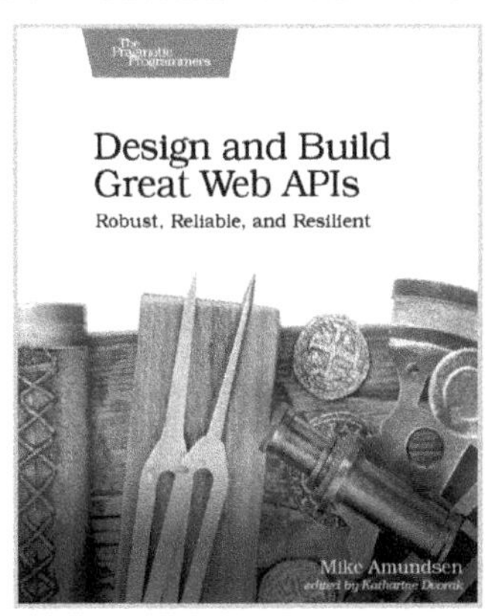

APIs are transforming the business world at an increasing pace. Gain the essential skills needed to quickly design, build, and deploy quality web APIs that are robust, reliable, and resilient. Go from initial design through prototyping and implementation to deployment of mission-critical APIs for your organization. Test, secure, and deploy your API with confidence and avoid the "release into production" panic. Tackle just about any API challenge with more than a dozen open-source utilities and common programming patterns you can apply right away.

Mike Amundsen
(330 pages) ISBN: 9781680506808. $45.95
https://pragprog.com/book/maapis

Quantum Computing

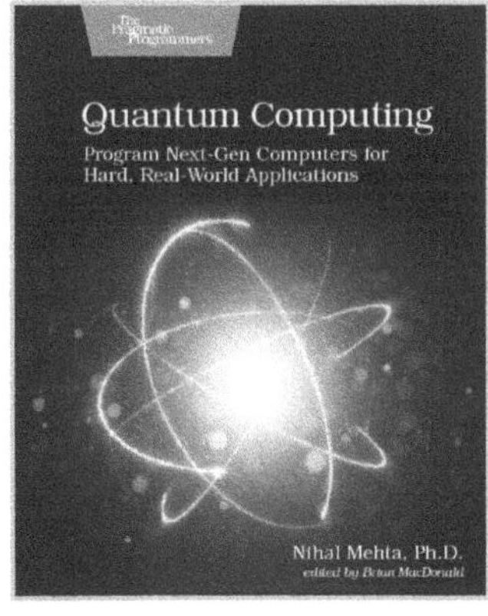

You've heard that quantum computing is going to change the world. Now you can check it out for yourself. Learn how quantum computing works, and write programs that run on the IBM Q quantum computer, one of the world's first functioning quantum computers. Develop your intuition to apply quantum concepts for challenging computational tasks. Write programs to trigger quantum effects and speed up finding the right solution for your problem. Get your hands on the future of computing today.

Nihal Mehta, Ph.D.
(580 pages) ISBN: 9781680507201. $45.95
https://pragprog.com/book/nmquantum

A Common-Sense Guide to Data Structures and Algorithms, Second Edition

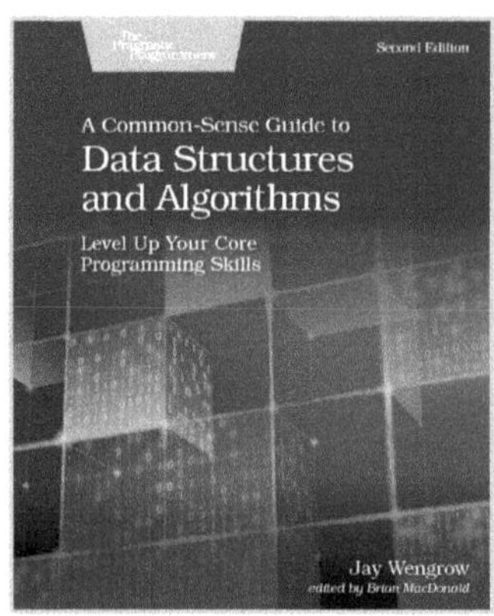

If you thought that data structures and algorithms were all just theory, you're missing out on what they can do for your code. Learn to use Big O Notation to make your code run faster by orders of magnitude. Choose from data structures such as hash tables, trees, and graphs to increase your code's efficiency exponentially. With simple language and clear diagrams, this book makes this complex topic accessible, no matter your background. This new edition features practice exercises in every chapter, and new chapters on topics such as dynamic programming and heaps and tries. Get the hands-on info you need to master data structures and algorithms for your day-to-day work.

Jay Wengrow
(506 pages) ISBN: 9781680507225. $45.95
https://pragprog.com/book/jwdsal2

Build Location-Based Projects for iOS

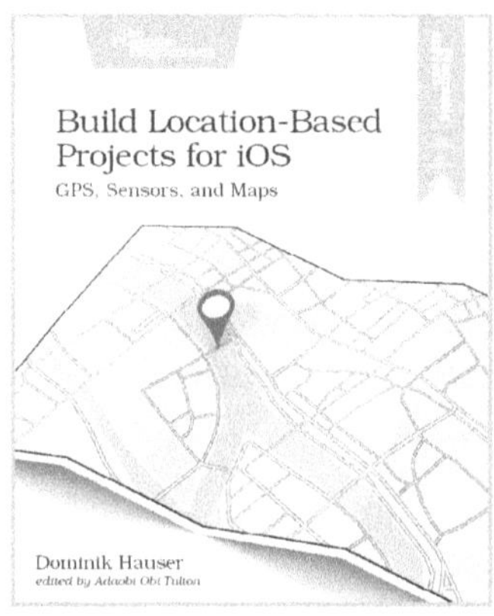

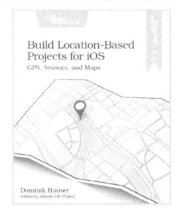

Coding is awesome. So is being outside. With location-based iOS apps, you can combine the two for an enhanced outdoor experience. Use Swift to create your own apps that use GPS data, read sensor data from your iPhone, draw on maps, automate with geofences, and store augmented reality world maps. You'll have a great time without even noticing that you're learning. And even better, each of the projects is designed to be extended and eventually submitted to the App Store. Explore, share, and have fun.

Dominik Hauser
(154 pages) ISBN: 9781680507812. $26.95
https://pragprog.com/book/dhios

iOS Unit Testing by Example

Fearlessly change the design of your iOS code with solid unit tests. Use Xcode's built-in test framework XCTest and Swift to get rapid feedback on all your code — including legacy code. Learn the tricks and techniques of testing all iOS code, especially view controllers (UIViewControllers), which are critical to iOS apps. Learn to isolate and replace dependencies in legacy code written without tests. Practice safe refactoring that makes these tests possible, and watch all your changes get verified quickly and automatically. Make even the boldest code changes with complete confidence.

Jon Reid
(358 pages) ISBN: 9781680506815. $47.95
https://pragprog.com/book/jrlegios

Become an Effective Software Engineering Manager

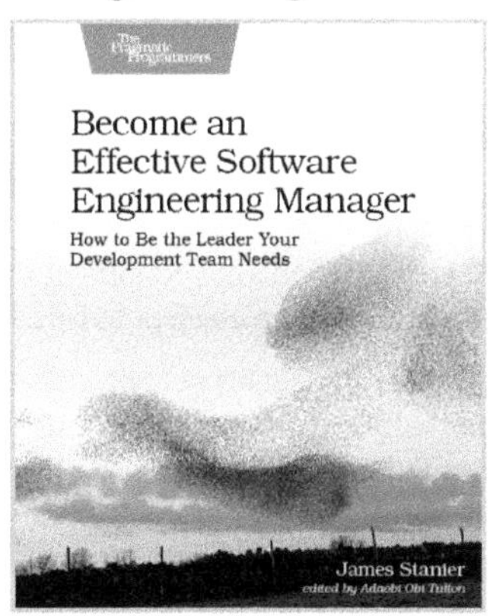

Software startups make global headlines every day. As technology companies succeed and grow, so do their engineering departments. In your career, you'll may suddenly get the opportunity to lead teams: to become a manager. But this is often uncharted territory. How do you decide whether this career move is right for you? And if you do, what do you need to learn to succeed? Where do you start? How do you know that you're doing it right? What does "it" even mean? And isn't management a dirty word? This book will share the secrets you need to know to manage engineers successfully.

James Stanier
(396 pages) ISBN: 9781680507249. $45.95
https://pragprog.com/book/jsengman

The Pragmatic Bookshelf

The Pragmatic Bookshelf features books written by professional developers for professional developers. The titles continue the well-known Pragmatic Programmer style and continue to garner awards and rave reviews. As development gets more and more difficult, the Pragmatic Programmers will be there with more titles and products to help you stay on top of your game.

Visit Us Online

This Book's Home Page

https://pragprog.com/book/tjgo

Source code from this book, errata, and other resources. Come give us feedback, too!

Keep Up to Date

https://pragprog.com

Join our announcement mailing list (low volume) or follow us on twitter @pragprog for new titles, sales, coupons, hot tips, and more.

New and Noteworthy

https://pragprog.com/news

Check out the latest pragmatic developments, new titles and other offerings.

Save on the ebook

Save on the ebook versions of this title. Owning the paper version of this book entitles you to purchase the electronic versions at a terrific discount.

PDFs are great for carrying around on your laptop—they are hyperlinked, have color, and are fully searchable. Most titles are also available for the iPhone and iPod touch, Amazon Kindle, and other popular e-book readers.

Send a copy of your receipt to support@pragprog.com and we'll provide you with a discount coupon.

Contact Us

Online Orders:	*https://pragprog.com/catalog*
Customer Service:	*support@pragprog.com*
International Rights:	*translations@pragprog.com*
Academic Use:	*academic@pragprog.com*
Write for Us:	*http://write-for-us.pragprog.com*
Or Call:	+1 800-699-7764

Milton Keynes UK
Ingram Content Group UK Ltd.
UKHW051316051024
449280UK00005B/14